Praise for

LENNON, DYLAN, ALICE, & JESUS

"God has given Greg Laurie a unique ministry of speaking to the people of whatever the current generation or culture may be—whether it was ten years ago, twenty, thirty, forty years ago, or today. He doesn't live inside 'the box'; therefore, his ministry remains fresh, reaching the multitudes of society. Thank You, Jesus, and thank you, Greg."

> **—Richie Furay,** founding member of Buffalo Springfield and Poco and Rock & Roll Hall of Fame inductee

"There's a big difference between success and fulfillment. Greg Laurie shows us in *Lennon, Dylan, Alice, & Jesus* how some choose to live in a higher reality and become fully alive. The stories are entertaining but full of substance."

> **—Dion DiMucci,** cofounder of Dion and the Belmonts, Rock & Roll Hall of Fame inductee, and Grammy Hall of Fame inductee

"Some of the greatest Christian artists of all time share their passionate stories and spiritual journeys that soar and crash in this book. What emerges are tales of godly frustration mixed with heartfelt dedication to God's purpose that eventually speak redemption and victory that touched masses of searching souls. The trials and triumphs of these righteous romantic rebels are reflected in the lyrics and melodies of their songs and the amazing events that surrounded young lives with purpose during a turbulent era of a fresh new music that glorified a risen Lord."

> **—Ken Mansfield,** former U.S. manager of Apple Records and author of *The Beatles, The Bible, and Bodega Bay* and *The Roof: The Beatles' Final Concert*

"Just when you think you know everything you ever need to know about the greatest music legends of our time, up pops *Lennon, Dylan, Alice, & Jesus* serving up a riveting feast of superbly-told anecdotes along with a powerful spiritual message to demonstrate that even our biggest heroes are mere mortals."

—**Ivor Davis,** author of award–winning *The Beatles and Me On Tour*

Lennon, Dylan, Alice, & Jesus

Lennon, Dylan, Alice, & Jesus

The Spiritual Biography of Rock and Roll

Greg Laurie
Marshall Terrill

SALEM
BOOKS

an imprint of Regnery Publishing
Washington, D.C.

CONTENTS

There will be three big surprises when we get to Heaven.

Some of the people we thought would be there won't be.

Some of the people we never thought would be there will be.

Because of God's faithful promises, you and I will also be there.

Introduction

It's time I admitted it . . . to quote the great theologian, Joan Jett, "I Love Rock 'n Roll."

Starting with Elvis Presley, my love for rock really took off when I heard the first strains of "I Wanna Hold Your Hand" from four young lads who came from a place I had never heard of before—a port city in England named Liverpool.

They were called the Beatles, and they literally impacted the world. Many musicians have acknowledged that they decided to start a band after first seeing "The Fab Four" in 1964 on a Sunday evening variety program called *The Ed Sullivan Show*.

Frankly, I wonder where all the rock bands have gone of late. I have had the privilege of personally meeting and getting to know a lot of rock icons over the years, and I have such great admiration for their talent. So yes, I admit it. I'm a fan.

But I am also a pastor, so you are probably wondering why I, of all people, am writing a book on rock stars, musicians, and their lives. I'm glad you asked! The reason I am writing this book is to look at the spiritual journeys of these iconic people who have entertained us for decades.

They have provided the soundtracks to our lives. A song can be played, and we are instantly transported to another time and even a specific moment. Many of these stars came to sad and even tragic ends. Others found hope and change in their lives. Still others are a work in progress. This is their story—and in many ways, it's our story, too.

I have already written three other spiritual biographies, one on "The King of Cool" himself, American film icon Steve McQueen. He had it all and then some. But he was dissatisfied, and he went on a search that ultimately changed his life.

Another is about the man they called "The Godfather of Cool" . . . the legendary Johnny Cash. His story is different than McQueen's in that Cash was raised as a Christian and was a believer from his childhood. He had many struggles over the years, but in the end, his faith was stronger than ever.

My most recent spiritual biography is about the man who impacted both McQueen and Cash: my own spiritual mentor, evangelist Billy Graham. Billy was a friend of Cash and was there for McQueen at a pivotal moment in his life.

These books came as a pleasant surprise to me in that I didn't plan to write about those figures; I was simply hit with a bout of inspiration.

And there are lot of surprises in this book.

Would you believe you will see some dreadlocked guy with tattoos on his face who plays death metal singing with the angels in Heaven? A guy with a snake hanging around his neck who beheads mannequins onstage? People who have done so many drugs they didn't even know where they were or which decade they were in? People who played in bands like the Byrds, Buffalo Springfield, Grand Funk Railroad, Foreigner, Poison, Metallica, Twisted

Sister, and Megadeth? *These* people are going to be in Heaven? I know there's no disease in Paradise, but Grandma's still going to have a heart attack if these guys show up there!

And what about the Beatles? They went to India and hung out with a long-haired and bearded guru who giggled a lot. They smoked a lot of pot and dropped a lot of acid, and John Lennon once said they were more popular than Jesus. What is their spiritual story?

Then there are the founding members of the 27 Club: Jimi Hendrix, Brian Jones, Janis Joplin, and Jim Morrison. They all died at that age. Hendrix said music was his religion. Joplin was a chef's salad of Southern Comfort, heroin, speed, and whatever else she could get her hands on, but she also loved painting, poetry, and literature. Morrison was the on-the-edge Lizard King, trying to turn Doors concerts into ecstatic ancient Greek rituals, but he also had an IQ of 149 and carefully listened to pastors who tried to engage him.

Bob Dylan is still among us, and he is truly an icon of rock and music. If there were a Mount Rushmore of musical legends, surly Robert Zimmerman (Dylan's real name) would be there. He was born and raised Jewish. Then he announced that he was a Christian, much to the shock and surprise of many.

Dylan recorded three albums that have strong biblical content, and since then, his faith has taken many twists and turns. He summed it up perfectly in one of his newer songs, "I Contain Multitudes." One of the most revealing lyrics is: "I'm a man of contradictions, I'm a man of many moods. I contain multitudes." I would describe him as a work in progress.

Fact is, everyone is a work in progress. You never know where or when a person changes in their life. The Bible says, "We live our lives like a story that's been told" (Psalm 90:9). For some, that story is not over; new chapters are being written. For others, that story has had a tragic ending. So much of this happens in secret. Behind the scenes. Many of these stars were raised in Christian homes but went astray in some way before finding their way back home. One of them just had to black out and hit four parked cars, then try to escape the police by crawling away in order to have his come-to-Jesus moment. (Free tip: the police will catch you if you get liquored up and try to crawl away from them.)

Though some see rock and roll as the antithesis of true faith, the truth is that many rock stars have become believers because they've lived at the pinnacle of an empty world and know that ultimately, it's not satisfying. There must be something to this, because leaving fame, fortune, and the easy life to take up the cross is no small choice.

I've explored the roots of these people's tales, and I'm going to share some things in this book you may never have heard before. For some stars, it will be a spiritual story that's never been told about them before. And that's rarely simple. (Did you know Alice Cooper almost died when he was thirteen? But he didn't commit his life to following Jesus Christ until he was thirty-five. Why? You'll learn in the pages that follow.) Along the way, we'll take a trip down memory lane to explore an informal history of rock music through the decades—including the genesis of Contemporary Christian Music. As you'll see, that is particularly dear to my heart.

Music icons are complicated, talented, driven people. They breathe rarified air. What they have accomplished is not easy—otherwise, everyone would do it. They clawed their way to the heights of a near-impossible field and succeeded.

But when they got to the top—the Olympic swimming pool, the pet tiger, the fifteen-bedroom mansion, the private jet—they found none of those things did it for them any longer. If they weren't dying, losing their minds, or dissolving into emotional mud puddles, they just got tired of it all.

What turned these rock stars to the Lord? Is there a common denominator? Are there even answers at all? We're going to explore a lot.

But whatever answers we find—or don't—know this: no one is beyond the reach of God.

• • •

The Bible tells an unforgettable parable you're likely familiar with. It's comprised of three separate accounts with a common theme of lost things: a lamb, a coin, and a son. In telling us this simple story, Jesus was telling us about Himself.

A shepherd risked his own life to find and retrieve a lamb that had wandered off—just a foolish critter who chased the next tasty patch of luscious grass until he realized he was completely lost. The shepherd knew enough about that animal to understand that if he didn't literally go out in the night to save him, the elements or predators would take him out. The shepherd searched for the lost sheep, and when he found the helpless creature, he celebrated.

In the second tale, a woman lost a special coin. It was apparently a component of the headband she wore on her wedding day, so losing it would be to her like losing a wedding ring would be to us. The woman swept her whole house to find the misplaced coin. This thing did not wander off—no rebellion here. It simply wasn't guarded as carefully as it should have been. Like the shepherd with the wayward sheep, the lady aggressively pursued what was lost—and when she found it after her relentless search, she celebrated.

In the third tale, the lost thing was a boy—a young man. He was the heir to a significant portion of his father's wealth, but he shamelessly insulted his father and demanded that he receive what was due him in advance and be turned loose from the bonds of familial obligation. The father granted his wish, and the boy marched into a wasteland of "riotous" living. (Sounds like some of these rocks stars you already know about, doesn't it?) The father eagerly waited for his son's return, and when the prodigal came home, there was a serious party.

You're going to read some amazing—and sometimes sad—stuff ahead. Some of these musicians wandered off into perilous territory, chasing one shiny thing after another until they were in no-man's-land. Others were abused—victims of the foolishness of their parents, family members, or "friends." And some shook their musical instruments in the face of the perfect, merciful Creator of the Universe, and stormed off.

But these three things—the sheep, the coin, and the lad—were returned home safely. The story these musicians would tell, if they could, is not about the mistakes and tragedies of their lives, but about the predictability of a God who loved them with the kind of grace we cannot imagine—a merciful God who welcomed them home.

You may not be a rock star with millions of dollars in royalties to squander on a lavish lifestyle, but with all respect, you are a lost thing. I am, too.

Yet, you and I have a Savior who does just as His title implies: He saves. He rescues lost things. He restores.

My prayer is that, regardless of where you are in your own story, the book that follows will be a reminder that this same God is seeking you. Relentlessly. Lovingly.

Welcome, and God bless you as He writes your story.

Greg Laurie
January 2022

CHAPTER ONE

The Gospel Roots of Rock 'n Roll

Some astrophysicists claim the universe started with a spontaneous explosion. A big bang.

Stars and planets were formed out of rock, minerals, and superheated gases. Different elements smashed into each other, coalesced, and created new bodies. Gravity held them together, and they drew new elements into their orbit.

You probably won't be shocked to hear that this isn't the origin story I subscribe to, but it makes for a decent metaphor. Music historians claim the rock and roll universe came together kind of like this.

It started with gospel which, in turn, gave birth to blues, then country and western. Swing and jazz followed, giving birth to rhythm and blues sometime in the 1940s. People called it "rock and roll spiritual singing." Like the idea of a solar system forming around a star over time, "rock and roll" slowly became a heavenly body unto itself. I use the term "heavenly" because the church is where many of rock's earliest stars got their inspiration and their start.

Shelby County, Tennessee, anchors neighboring Arkansas, Mississippi, and the boot heel of Missouri. Seated at the top of the Chickasaw Bluffs above the Mississippi River, Memphis was one of the largest cities of the Old South and a marketplace for crops, lumber, and cotton. It was a laborer's city. People worked from sunrise to sunset six days a week. The seventh day was devoted to church, music, and food. Out in the cotton fields, which supplied the entire country, workers sang hymns to make the drudgery pass by more quickly. Tennessee was, after all, the "Bible Belt"—and the belt was cinched real tight.

The few hours people had away from the fields each week were often spent in church. Even the poorest had "Sunday best" to wear. Sermonizers were often preachers who rained down hellfire and damnation on their searching listeners. They instilled such a fear of God that men stayed sober and children behaved the rest of the day. Traveling preachers—better known as evangelists or revivalists, with their theatrical gestures and oratorical gymnastics, often holding court under a tent or brush arbor—provided a break from the local pastor. Afterward, everyone celebrated with picnics, where they feasted on barbecue, ham, greens (always cooked with bacon), black-eyed peas, biscuits, and pie. It was undoubtedly the best meal these folks consumed all week.

Elvis Presley, Johnny Cash, Jerry Lee Lewis, and Carl Perkins were all church-going country boys from impoverished, hard-working families, many of whom had alcoholism and addiction in their blood. Jerry Lee Lewis came from a poor East Louisiana farm family. Elvis Presley in Mississippi, Carl Perkins in Tennessee, and Johnny Cash in Arkansas all grew up in the hardscrabble homes of sharecroppers. Often starting as early as age six, they worked in the fields and chipped in financially whenever they could to help their families survive. School was secondary to work, almost a luxury. Some, like Cash and Perkins, grew up in "shotgun shacks" on dirt roads while others, like Elvis, came of age in government housing projects in the inner city where gangs, fist-fighting, petty theft, and bad habits were a normal part of childhood.

"The older kids took it upon themselves to make the younger kids tough, and often that meant making us fight each other," said Sonny West, who grew up in the Lamar Terrace neighborhood of southeast Memphis, not far from where Presley lived when the family moved to Tennessee. He later became Elvis's bodyguard. "What it boiled down to was that you were either going to survive by doing what it took, or you were going to get beat up."[1]

It was a life that permanently scarred everyone who lived it.

Sin, guilt, and unrelenting hardship made for a heavy bottle to be nursed on. These four young men all came up that hard way, and the pressures they grew up with built until they exploded into a new sound.

Most genres of American music have emanated from a specific city. Seattle is where grunge started. The Motown sound originated in Detroit. Country rock was born in Los Angeles. Rap evolved from New York's inner city. And rock 'n roll was founded in Memphis, along with gospel and rockabilly.

This was the perfect place for it. The great W. C. Handy, often referred to as "The Father of the Blues," recorded there. Electric guitars transformed the acoustic Mississippi Delta Sound into post-war American blues. Blacks and whites both listened to the new music for the same reasons: it liberated something inside them. While Tennessee was still part of the Jim Crow South, there's no doubt that black music influenced white artists—and none more so than the "King of Rock 'n Roll," Elvis Aaron Presley.

Presley grew up in Tupelo, Mississippi, in a small, two-bedroom house nestled among a group of small, rough-hewn homes along Old Saltillo Road. The house had no electricity and sat at the edge of a ramshackle neighborhood called Shake Rag. The music that came out of Shake Rag's house parties, restaurants, jukeboxes, and churches influenced Elvis' musical development.

"Some people say Elvis never heard black music, but he sure did. You couldn't *not* hear it," recalled Billy Smith, Presley's first cousin, in reference to Shake Rag. "The walls were so thin you'd hear 'em from the outside. Or they'd be on the front porch singing. That's where Elvis picked up on a lot of it."[2]

Presley was also greatly influenced by his parents . . . and the church.

"My mother and dad both loved to sing," he once said. "They tell me when I was three or four years old, I got away from them and walked in front of the choir and I was beating time."[3]

Johnny Cash—known to his family as J. R.—got his musical leanings from the cotton fields, his church, and radio. His sister, Joanne Cash Yates, recalled the family had a battery-powered radio bought from Sears, Roebuck & Co. for the living room at home, and the whole family listened to music and programs such as *Gangbusters, Inner Sanctum, The Squeaking Door,* and *Suppertime Frolics.*

"The *Grand Ole Opry* on Saturday night was a real treat for us," she said. "J. R. and I would sit facing each other in straight-back chairs while brothers Jack and Tommy and my sisters would listen as well."[4]

After the death of his fifteen-year-old brother, Jack, in a freak shop accident, twelve-year-old J. R. turned more inward. He started composing poetry and bought a guitar. His mother and a childhood friend taught him songs, mostly country tunes. Later, gospel began to color his sound. He was especially moved by American recording artist Sister Rosetta Tharpe, who combined spiritual lyrics with the electric guitar, which contributed greatly to the genesis of rock and roll.

In the small town of Ferriday, Louisiana, Jerry Lee Lewis began playing the piano with two cousins—Mickey Gilley and Jimmy Swaggart—in his youth. His parents mortgaged their farm to get him that piano. Turns out, it was a great investment.

Lewis gave his first public performance at fourteen, playing with a country and western band at a car dealership. Though his mother enrolled him at the Bible Institute in Waxahachie, Texas so he could sing gospel songs, he later said his biggest musical influences came from an older cousin who played piano and exposed him to the radio and acts at Haney's Big House—a juke joint on the other side of the tracks.

The morning after he played a boogie-woogie version of "My God Is Real" at a school assembly, the dean kicked him out of the Bible Institute. Apparently the devil had a new minion, and the world had some killer songs.

Presley, Cash, and Lewis were all solidly middle-class compared to the Perkins family, who were so poor that there was no farm to mortgage for purchasing a piano or ordering a guitar from Sears, Roebuck & Co. Carl's daddy made his first instrument, a cigar-box-and-broomstick guitar. It was hillbilly luthiery at its finest.

Perkins heard Southern gospel music in church on Sundays and the rest of the week from African American cotton pickers. At age fourteen, he got his first paying gig at a roadside tavern notorious for being the scene of frequent fistfights. Despite being underage, Perkins was paid in liquor, so he drank four beers his first night. He ended up throwing back more beer as a youngster than most people drink in their lifetimes . . . and as you'd guess, in time, this became a real problem.

These four were stars being born—and beginning to shine bright, but they needed a dimmed place to illuminate—a place that would cement their names in a galaxy. That place was Memphis, Tennessee.

Memphis in the 1950s was a city in transition. It was a shipping hub, but the cotton and textile industries still dominated. Segregation was rigid, as it was elsewhere in the Deep South. The suburbs were beginning to sprout, and music was a large part of the city's culture. Beale Street was still the center of the Memphis music scene, as it had been since the 1860s when traveling black musicians began performing there because it was a thriving area of commerce and culture. It was the symbolic capital of black Memphis, but whites adopted it as their entertainment district. It was culturally (not politically) desegregated. Elvis often wandered around Beale Street in his teenage years, buying clothes and taking in the sights and sounds of this vibrant place; B. B. King said it was there that he struck up an acquaintance with "The King."

However, the most important institution that opened on Beale Street wasn't a nightclub; it was an obscure little enterprise in a squat concrete building at 706 Union Avenue called Memphis Recording Service. Started in 1950, its owner, a twenty-seven-year-old entrepreneur named Sam Phillips, saw it as a way to record and promote some of the local blues music that flowed from the venues lining the block.

On Saturday, June 13, 1953, Elvis Presley was an eighteen-year-old who had recently graduated from Memphis's Humes High School when, on a whim, he dropped by Phillips's place to record a pair of songs on a ten-inch acetate: "My Happiness" and "That's When Your Heartaches Begin." His baritone voice (with tenor qualities) caught the attention of Marion Keisker, a studio manager under Phillips, who encouraged Elvis to come back to the studio so her boss could make an assessment. For years, Phillips had been hunting for a white artist who sounded like a black singer. Phillips figured if he could find that, he'd make a million dollars.

Elvis thought his voice was meant for something else. He originally wanted to become a gospel singer, and when he appeared on *The Ed Sullivan Show* as he was peaking as the first real "rock star," he sang "Peace in the Valley" because it was one of his mother's favorite hymns. Elvis's friend Jerry Schilling noted, "Anytime Elvis was going through a really rough time, he always retreated to gospel music."

Studio sessions with Presley were hopelessly unfruitful until the evening of July 5, 1954. He and two local musicians, Scotty Moore and Bill Black, had been striking out all night. They were about to pack up and go home when Elvis picked up his guitar and lit into a blues number from the 1940s called "That's All Right (Mama)." He'd first heard the number penned by Arthur "Big Boy" Crudup coming out of a juke joint in Shake Rag, and it had stuck with him. He was jumping around, "acting the fool" according to Moore, when Black picked up his bass and started following along. That's when Phillips stuck his head out of the control room and asked, "What are you doing?"

"We don't know," they answered.

Phillips told them to back up, find a place to start, and do it again. The result was the sound he had been looking for all those years.[5]

"That's All Right (Mama)" was a regional smash in the South, even though it was too black for country music and too hillbilly for rhythm and blues. "I didn't know what to make of it," Roy Orbison said. "There was just no reference point in the culture to compare it."[6]

That's because a seismic shift was about to take place in popular music. Rock and roll was being birthed.

Once "That's All Right (Mama)" started getting heavy airplay throughout the South, Elvis wannabes streamed through the front and back doors of the newly named, and soon-to-be world-famous, Sun Records. Marion Keisker's phone jangled from the time she reported to work till she closed the door and went home, with all the callers pleading to audition for Sam Phillips. One of the most persistent was a twenty-two-year-old Air Force veteran named Johnny Cash, who was usually told Phillips was out of town or in conference. One time, he got lucky, and Phillips himself answered the phone, but as soon as Cash introduced himself as a gospel singer, the Sun Records mogul winced. He told Cash that gospel music was nice but not marketable. Goodbye.

Cash eventually won Phillips over enough to land an audition, during which he played a variety of country and rockabilly songs. He would ultimately distinguish himself as one of the "Kings of Country Music" while Elvis was the "King of Rock 'n Roll."

But in his heart, Johnny was, first and foremost, a gospel singer.

Meanwhile, Carl Perkins had no misconceptions about who he was. He always viewed himself as a brawling rockabilly artist. He and Cash struck up a fast friendship and often bounced ideas off each other. Cash proved to be a helpful sounding board for Perkins as the latter worked on "Blue Suede Shoes," offering encouragement and suggestions. Phillips, however, gave the song to Elvis, who reluctantly recorded it. Perkins's signature song turned out to be a smash hit for Elvis, far outselling the Perkins version. It also helped propel Presley's stardom, leaving Perkins in the dust.

"Elvis had everything," Perkins said. "He had the looks, the moves, the manager, and the talent. And he didn't look like Mr.

Ed, like a lot of us did. Elvis was hitting them with sideburns, flashy clothes, and no ring on the finger. I had three kids."[7]

Jerry Lee Lewis entered the Sun Studio sphere as a session player for several artists, including Perkins and Billy Lee Riley. He signed a solo deal in 1956, and the next year became a breakout artist with hits such as "Great Balls of Fire" and "Whole Lotta Shakin' Going On." Known as "The Killer," Lewis had a temper and personality that were as volatile as his famous flaming piano. He drunkenly crashed his Lincoln Continental into the gates of Graceland, asking to see Elvis; killed a horse with his Buick; waged war on producers; accidentally shot his bass player; and married seven women, including his thirteen-year-old third cousin. And that's just a shallow dive into what can genteelly be described as a colorful life.

On December 4, 1956, four of the greatest stars in American music happened to be together in the same recording studio at the same time. The sessions became known as the "Million Dollar Quartet"—for obvious reasons.

The dollar amount is often cited as a rough guess at what it would have cost to pay these four men to sing together. It was Presley, Cash, Lewis, and Perkins. Perkins was in the studio that day cutting new tracks. Lewis backed him on piano. Cash was there, having dropped in to watch Perkins. Meanwhile, up front, Presley dropped in on Phillips to say hello. Phillips led Presley into the studio, and the four started an impromptu jam session. All Phillips had to do was leave the tape running, and that's exactly what he did. They recorded nearly four dozen tunes, almost half of which were gospel. Others were rock and roll classics like "Blue Suede Shoes," "Long Tall Sally," "I Walk the Line," and "Great Balls of Fire."

If this were Europe in the late 1700s, it would be like having Beethoven, Handel, Mozart, and Tchaikovsky in one room at the same time. All four of those men became legends. All four had their own trajectories. All four had their own battles. And all four eventually came to their own spiritual reckoning.

Of the four, Elvis's star burned the brightest and the fastest. He never lost sight of his Savior, but he did lose sight of himself, courtesy of an addiction to pills that turned him into a caricature of himself. He was introduced to them in the Army, used them to stay slim during his movie years, and abused them when he began touring again in 1969. A few years later, he began to slowly unravel, then spiral quickly out of control. He died in 1977 at the age of forty-two.

In the late 1950s, Elvis was drafted into the U.S. Army. He spent almost two years in Germany, and when he returned to America in 1960, the music scene had changed. He tried to adapt and soon found himself in a series of films that went from bad to worse. When he wasn't working, he explored the mysteries of yoga, tai chi, Scientology, reincarnation, and transcendental meditation. He also studied Kabbalah, Taoism, Buddhism, Judaism, and Christianity. He sometimes wore the Star of David and the cross at the same time. When questioned by the media or an acquaintance, he joked he wore both so he wouldn't be kept out of Heaven on a technicality.

"All I want to know is the truth, to know and experience God," Presley once said. "I'm a searcher, that's what I'm all about."[8]

When rock was at its zenith in 1967 and the Beatles, the Rolling Stones, and Jimi Hendrix were becoming the new rave, Elvis released a gospel album, *How Great Thou Art*. The singing was inspired and showed where his heart was.

"Elvis was always looking for answers. Why him?" said his wife, Priscilla Presley. "Maybe God had something else for him. Am I supposed to be giving some kind of message?" She said his "go-to" song was "Take My Hand, Precious Lord."[9]

I am tired, I'm weak, I am worn through the storm
Let me on to the light, take me home, precious Lord
Lead me home

Near the end of his life, Elvis was in turmoil. He had run out of mountains to climb and he was burned out artistically. He turned to prescription drugs to ease that pain.

"(Elvis) had a lot of problems. Isolation that brings on drug abuse. It had to be very lonely. We know that," said singer-songwriter Tom Petty. "There's a point where you have success, when you are wealthy, and there is that day when the letter comes that none of this is going to make me happy. And he knew he had to try and find something, you know? I think he felt out-gunned and gave up."[10] Ironically, Tom Petty would die of a drug overdose almost forty years after Elvis's demise.

Presley never forgot his place in the grand order of things. One of my favorite stories about him took place when he was performing in Las Vegas sometime in the 1970s. During the show, a woman approached the stage carrying a pillow on which rested a crown.

"It's for you," she told Elvis. "You're the king."

Elvis took her hand in his, smiled, and said, "No, honey, there is only one King, and His name is Jesus Christ. I'm just a singer."[11]

Whenever fans told Elvis they "worshipped" him, he would kindly ask them to "love my music, but don't ever worship anyone but the Lord."

. . .

Johnny Cash was also a searcher. He was searching for peace between the dual poles of his conflicted personality.

"Sometimes I am two people," Cash said. "Johnny is the nice one. Cash causes all the trouble. They fight."[12]

Indeed, they did. His body and mind were a battlefield his entire life. He was often embroiled in scandal or controversy stemming from high-profile arrests, car accidents, and other drug-and-alcohol-induced escapades, including one resulting in a forest fire that thoroughly scorched more than five hundred acres. His music and social activism gave light and hope to others, but Cash's dark side often overruled his true nature.

He started and finished well, both musically and spiritually. He stands as a textbook example of a man who found that, by His grace, God gives second chances in life.

Carl Perkins experienced that second chance in late 1967.

* * *

Many say his drinking got out of control in late March 1956. That's when Perkins was in a horrific car accident that put him in the hospital for several months. The accident near Wilmington, Delaware, also killed his manager and eventually claimed the life of his brother, Jay. Perkins survived but woke up in obscurity. He was relegated to opening for Johnny Cash on tour when he should have been headlining his own shows.

So one night in 1967, he warmed up for Cash in front of several thousand fans in Los Angeles's Shrine Auditorium. He blazed through his set smashed on a fifth of whiskey, hoping no one would notice. Perkins had been drunk for four consecutive days, and his alcoholism was literally eating him alive.

The next morning, he woke up in the back of Cash's tour bus, parked in a lot near the Pacific Ocean, feeling like he'd already died. He confessed as much to June Carter, who was part of the touring troupe.

"I don't deserve to live. I ought to die," Perkins cried. "God can't love me anymore."

"Oh, yes, He does," Carter replied. "You talk to Him. John and I'll let you be. When you feel up to it, come join us and the others."

Perkins staggered out of the bus and found a spot on the ocean sand. He drifted in and out of consciousness for a long time. He was sick to his stomach, his head was spinning, and he was experiencing delirium tremens, the most severe form of alcohol withdrawal. He began to pray.

"Lord, I don't have the right to ask You to let me live, but Lord, if I'm dying, let me live long enough to see Val [his wife] and my little kids. Let them see me sober, but don't let me die here, like this."[13]

When Perkins got back on the bus, he marched right toward his brown tote bag and pulled out a pint of whiskey. As he lifted the bottle to his lips, he heard an audible voice say,

"Carl, you asked Me to let you make it home, but if you take one drink, you'll never see your family again."

Those words shook him to his core.

Perkins mustered the strength to walk back to the beach and toss the bottle into the Pacific Ocean. It took three skips before it sank. He returned to the bus, where he was met by Cash, who had his own battles with a different kind of bottle—a brown prescription bottle. Cash made Perkins a promise.

"You don't take a drink, I don't take a pill," he said.[14]

Perkins made it through the rest of the tour and sobered up. He eventually rededicated his life to Christ and remained a Christian until his death in 1998. He and Cash struggled with their sobriety for the rest of their lives, but their faith was bedrock.

. . .

Presley, Cash, and Perkins all had conflicts between the warring elements of their personalities, between themselves and addiction, and between the push and pull of fame. But Jerry Lee Lewis fought his entire life over his faith and "the devil's music" that he loved to play. He initially refused to record "Great Balls of Fire" because he considered it blasphemous. Throughout his lifetime, Lewis repeatedly said he found himself falling short of the glory of God.

In the 1970s, he was discussing "Jesus Rock" being played in churches when he said, "The difference is I know I am playing for the devil, and they don't."[15]

These days, Lewis is singing a different tune. In a 2015 interview with *The Guardian* when he was eighty years old, Lewis wondered about his soul. He doesn't worry about the music anymore; it's the lifestyle he thinks was ungodly. He is certain he knows where his talent came from.

"How could it be the devil's music?" he wondered. "Satan didn't give me the talent. God gave me the talent, and I've always told people that."[16]

Elvis Presley, Johnny Cash, Carl Perkins, and Jerry Lee Lewis—true pioneers of rock and roll—were all church-going country boys who believed in Jesus, but the devil seduced their souls and didn't let go for decades. However, they eventually found their way back to the Light and rolled in His glory.

CHAPTER TWO

More Popular
than Jesus

Like millions of other Americans, I first noticed the Beatles when they made their historic appearance on *The Ed Sullivan Show* on a Sunday night in early February 1964. What made it so significant was the fact that 73 million people were watching. The country's population was only 192 million at the time. That's almost 40 percent of all Americans. Nobody gets those kinds of numbers these days.

At the time of the broadcast, I was twelve years old and living with my grandparents, Stella and Charles McDaniel, in South Gate, California. We watched the show faithfully each week, along with *Bonanza* and *Wanted: Dead or Alive*, on their large black-and-white TV. I can close my eyes and still see and hear Mr. Sullivan declare, "We're going to have a really big *shew* tonight . . ."

The Beatles had quite a buildup leading into the appearance. "I Wanna Hold Your Hand" was issued as a single on January 1, 1964, by Capitol Records (remember the cool yellow and orange swirl logo?) and occupied the No. 1 spot for seven weeks. It was followed in quick succession by their debut album *Meet the Beatles!* and a slew of other singles ("She Loves You," "Please Please Me," and "I Saw Her Standing There," the B-side to "I Wanna Hold Your Hand.") Music and popular culture hadn't seen such a seismic shift since Elvis Presley appeared on the scene almost a decade before.

I immediately loved their music, which did not sound like any of the music of our day. Not remotely. When you go from "Puff the Magic Dragon" by Peter, Paul and Mary, "Roses are Red" by Bobby Vinton, or "Venus" by Frankie Avalon to "I Wanna Hold Your Hand," that's a seismic shift. It's like going from taking the city bus with Grandma to firing up the latest Ford Mustang convertible with the top down and your best friend riding along.

Their music was alive and vital, and I fell in love with this band from a mysterious place called Liverpool, England. They might as well have been from another planet. At the time, we did not know how much the Beatles were influenced by American artists like Buddy Holly, Roy Orbison, the Everly Brothers, Chuck Berry, Little Richard, Motown, and of course, Elvis Presley. They had a sound all their own.

And they looked different, too. They did not sport the Elvis Presley/James Dean combed-back-and-slicked-down ducktail. Their hair was longer, shaggy, and combed down. My grandparents, like many other authority figures of that time, felt these boys needed a serious haircut. (I, on the other hand, immediately wanted to grow my hair out just like them.)

Along with their matching suits and thick accents, the fact that they played their own instruments and wrote their own songs truly set them apart. They did not have a solo lead singer, as with Elvis or Frankie Valli. John Lennon and Paul McCartney shared the microphone and were the primary lead singers, trading vocals back and forth with an occasional lead vocal from lead guitarist George Harrison or drummer Ringo Starr. Everything about them was so cool and different and completely unique.

Add to this the fact that they were genuinely funny. They had been influenced by a British comedy program featuring Peter Sellers called *The Goon Show*. In fact, the radio show was produced by none other than George Martin, who would later become known as "The Fifth Beatle." This band of four working-class boys changed music and culture forever.

They also had impeccable timing. The Beatles came along as the country was still mourning the loss of President John F. Kennedy, who had been assassinated weeks before on November 22, 1963. He was forty-three when he was sworn into office. Young, handsome, and confident, he declared America was going to eliminate injustice, inequality, tyranny, and even send a man to the moon. With his beautiful and stylish wife, Jackie, at his side along with their children, Caroline and John, their arrival in Washington, D.C. was both a political and cultural shift. America, the "New Frontier," was not going to rest on its laurels during his presidency. We believed him, too. The country was finally free from the aftermath of World War II and the Korean War. Everyone—especially the youth—felt hopeful about the future.

Then he was taken away from us in the blink of an eye.

But only a few months after that horror, as if on cue, something fresh, different, and fun caught the nation's attention: an act on a popular television variety show.

The Beatles became instant stars after their appearance on *The Ed Sullivan Show* and triggered a form of adulation and unfathomable fame that produced ear-splitting screaming from teenaged girls and even a few boys. It was called "Beatlemania," and it tumbled out at us through radio, television, film, music, and even merchandising. Nothing quite like it had ever happened before. At any Woolworth's or large department store, you could buy Beatles hats, toys, buttons, trading cards, lunch boxes, figurines, and the Beatles wig, which had become the hottest novelty item since the yo-yo. Kids wore them to emulate their idols, and fun-loving parents plopped them on their own heads and instantly became the life of the party.

As a kid on the verge of my teen years, my budget was limited. However, I did manage to collect every Beatles album from *Meet the Beatles!* to *Let It Be*, and everything in between. I not only listened to their songs over and over, I studied the photos, the credits on the sleeves, and later memorized the lyrics from the liner notes. The Beatles are still a great case study for anyone who examines popular music because more than a half-century after they broke up, no one has been able to touch them in terms of musicality or popularity.

I have a large photo of the Beatles in my office and a young person seeing it recently asked me why I am such a fan. I told him they effectively provided the soundtrack of my life. Every song brings memories of my childhood, both good and bad. There were many other artists and bands I listened to growing up, but no single band impacted me the way those four lads from Liverpool did.

They have set the bar so high that no one in this lifetime will be able to come close. And that was only their beginning. A piece of art so transcendent in its every facet, like the *Sgt. Pepper's Lonely Hearts Club Band* album, was still far in their future.

Back then, they were still the often comical and charming mop-topped men with boyish grins and funny accents. And they rode the wave into the pop culture stratosphere with concerts and television appearances, fresh music, and movies. They made the girls scream and watched the money flood in, and all was well.

Then the culture shifted beneath them. President Kennedy had gotten us involved in the Vietnam War, President Johnson escalated it, and soon thousands of young American men were losing their lives. Images of full body bags helicoptered live from the battlefield poisoned the airwaves. This was followed by drugs and civil rights protests dominating the national argument. Beatles manager Brian Epstein, a highly conscious and sensitive man, muzzled them when it came to the press.

Be funny and charming, he told them, and don't talk about anything other than your favorite color or the last time you cut your hair. But when they began promoting their 1966 tour, they started talking about desegregation and the escalation of the Vietnam War. In March 1966, Lennon took it to another level. He told Maureen Cleave of the *Evening Standard*: "Christianity will go. It will vanish and shrink. I needn't argue about that; I'm right and will prove to be right. We're more popular than Jesus Christ right now. I don't know which will go first—Christianity or rock 'n roll. Jesus was alright, but His disciples were thick and ordinary. It's them twisting it that ruins it for me."[1]

On its face, Lennon had a point. For many young people in America, there was more excitement and passion for the Beatles than for Jesus. Churches of that day were largely out of touch, culturally speaking, and many American teenagers, instead of reading the words of the Apostles John and Paul, were more tuned in to another John and Paul . . . and George and Ringo.

Lennon's provocative statement created an instant firestorm across America. Especially in the South.

Radio stations and local pastors encouraged young people to bring their Beatles records to church and set them on fire in the parking lot. Some did. The images of these vinyl burnings stayed etched in the country's consciousness for a long time.

And yet, the Beatles were not anti-God. In fact, they were all raised with some form of Christian upbringing. These were Church of England choir boys. They had been peach-cheeked lads in choir stalls, singing classic Anglican hymns like "All Praise to Thee, My God, This Night" and "For All the Saints," while wearing cassocks, surplices, and tippets. I've been to England many times and always enjoyed its rich traditions. How did the Beatles' spiritual path start with mossy walls and Victorian hymns, then take a trip through Funky Town with explorations of Hinduism, Transcendental Meditation, Krishna consciousness, and New Age-type leanings?

All four Beatles were associated with either the Protestant (Lennon), Roman Catholic (Harrison and McCartney), or Evangelical Anglican (Starr) church in their childhood, but they had abandoned their religious upbringings by the time they conquered the music world.

In February 1965, the four members of the Beatles told *Playboy* magazine they were "agnostic, but not anti-religion."

"If you say you don't believe in God, everybody assumes you're anti-religious, and you probably think that's what we mean by that," Lennon said. "We're not quite sure what we are, but I know that we're more agnostic than atheist."[2]

A few months later while in the Bahamas filming a segment for *Help!*, their second feature film, there was a hint that they were open to learning about different cultures and religions. That's when they were introduced to Indian culture, philosophy, and yoga.

"We were in the Bahamas filming a section and a little yogi runs over to us," Lennon recalled. "We didn't know what they were in those days, and this little Indian guy comes legging over and gives us a book each, signed to us, on yoga. We didn't look at it, we just stuck it along with all the other things people would give us."[3]

There was also an introduction to Indian music which, in turn, led to an exploration of Far East religions. The Beatles were waiting to shoot a scene in an Indian restaurant where a few musicians were playing in the background. Harrison was intrigued by these men and their instruments, including a sitar, which had a pear-shaped body, a long, hollow throat, and a twenty-string, arched, moveable neck. It was hard to hold, but Harrison thought it produced an unusual and appealing sound.

He played the sitar on *Rubber Soul*'s "Norwegian Wood" and wanted to master the instrument. He felt that he got lucky on that track; he found the proper notes and it fit. But he wanted to learn more about the sitar and play better. He was told a musician named Ravi Shankar (father of Norah Jones) could help him achieve that goal. Harrison immediately went out, bought a Shankar album, and placed the needle of the record player on the vinyl grooves. The sound that came out of the speakers changed his life and so did the man, whom he finally met in June 1966.

"I could meet anybody. I could go in all the film stars' houses and meet Elvis and everybody, and we met a lot of really good people, but I never met one person who really impressed me," Harrison said. "The first person who impressed me in my life was Ravi Shankar, and he was the only person who didn't try to impress me."[4]

The two men met at a dinner party in London, and Shankar was skeptical. Pop stars holding and playing classical Indian instruments? Hmm—hard to envision anything productive coming out of a possible musical pairing. However, he sensed Harrison's sincerity and ultimately agreed to tutor him.

"I found he really wanted to learn," Shankar said in *Raga*, a 1971 documentary about the sitarist. "I never thought our meeting would cause such an explosion, that Indian music would suddenly appear on the pop scene."[5]

The explosion Shankar referred to was the cross-fertilization of Eastern religion and music with the Western world, which became prevalent in the late '60s and early '70s popular culture.

In September 1966, less than a month after the Beatles' last live performance at Candlestick Park in San Francisco, California, Harrison and his wife, model Pattie Boyd, flew to Bombay, India. The Beatle was eager to take sitar lessons with Shankar, visit temples, study yoga, and meet potential gurus. The layers and sounds and colors and noises of the country bombarded his senses, and Harrison fully immersed himself in it.

"The difference over here is that their religion is every second and every minute of their lives," he later said of that visit.[6]

In Shankar, Harrison found a mentor; next, he went looking for a guru. And the other Beatles tagged along.

With their touring obligations behind them, the Beatles had more time to record and enjoy their lives. They attended art openings, movie premieres, concerts, plays, and took in the culture of Swingin' Sixties London. They also began to explore solo projects to satisfy some of their individual artistic needs.

Lennon filmed a Dick Lester dark comedy in Spain called *How I Won the War*. (Lester also directed the first two Beatles films.) McCartney went on an African safari and composed a film soundtrack called *The Family Way*. Harrison took a trip to San Francisco's Haight-Ashbury district to see what the Summer of Love was all about. He also scored *Wonderwall Music*, all Indian-style compositions for a hippie movie of the same name. Ringo Starr and his wife, Maureen, opted to keep a lower profile. They bought a large mock Tudor home in Surrey, England, which they named "Sunny Heights." The six-bedroom home housed a private pub above the garage called The Flying Cow, which had a mirrored bar, pool table, and television. The Starrs entertained all three Beatles and a cadre of English rock stars and actors, including Peter Sellers. A go-kart track was also laid on the grounds.

During this period of fecundity, the Beatles shot a slew of promo videos (the precursor to MTV videos), wrote and recorded the double A-sided single "Strawberry Fields Forever" and "Penny Lane," shortly followed by the classic FM-rock album *Sgt. Pepper's Lonely Hearts Club Band*. They also produced the experimental film and soundtrack for *Magical Mystery Tour* (the one-hour movie was considered their first official flop), followed by a trip to Greece for a group summer vacation. They sailed down the coast from Athens looking for an island to buy.

"John and I were on acid all the time, sitting on the front of the ship playing ukuleles," Harrison recalled. "Greece was on the left; a big island was on the right. The sun was shining, and we sang 'Hare Krishna' for hours and hours."[7]

When they got back to England, they started laying the groundwork for Apple, their record label and multimedia company that had divisions for clothing, technology, music, film, and publishing. It was as ambitious and daring as they were.

Movie sets, African safaris, English country mansion parties, hobnobbing with celebrities, setting up a business empire, Greek cruises, island shopping—an extraordinary person might do one of these things in their whole life. This quartet did them all in a short time. They packed a lot of living into those days.

When you're able to simply wish yourself into the company of any famous person you can name, you might not feel a need to seek God because you're living like a god yourself. Everything the Beatles touched turned to gold. For any other rock star, this would have been the period when the fame takes over and the work turns to junk. Instead, the Beatles put out *Sgt. Pepper's Lonely Hearts Club Band*, their most highly acclaimed work to date.

In the wake of the *Magical Mystery Tour* film debacle and the death of their longtime manager, Brian Epstein, the band needed a new direction. They hoped a long-haired, bushy-bearded guru from India might give them spiritual guidance and slip them "The Answer."

Harrison, Lennon, and McCartney attended a lecture by the Maharishi Mahesh Yogi at the Hilton Hotel in London in August 1967. Harrison heard about his visit through his wife, Pattie. He needed a mantra and thought the white-robed guru who sat cross-legged and giggled an awful lot might just give him one. The Beatles landed front-row seats, of course, and enjoyed the lecture. They later met with the yogi in his hotel suite, reporting to him that, despite all their worldly success, they were seeking a highly spiritual experience. He told them Transcendental Meditation (TM) was their answer. They agreed to attend a ten-day conference in Wales and, a few months later, a three-month course for Westerners who wanted to become TM instructors. For that, they had to travel to the Maharishi's ashram in Rishikesh, India, which they did in February 1968.

The musicians brought their wives and significant others, fully intending to complete the course at the Maharishi's Academy of Transcendental Meditation. Starr not only brought his wife, but a good supply of Heinz baked beans. He had an ultra-sensitive stomach from a bout with peritonitis as a kid and found Indian spices and curries too harsh for his digestive system.

The Beatles' quest for spiritual enlightenment wasn't as profound as it was cracked up to be, said Ken Mansfield, who was the U.S. manager for Apple Records under The Fab Four and a high-ranking executive at Capitol Records.

"To be perfectly honest with you, I think the reason why they went to India was because it was a cool thing to do," Mansfield said. "George was very serious about his spiritual journey, but I think the others just went along because it was cool. And as you can see, they all dropped away quickly. They never felt the Maharishi had much of an influence on their lives after that."[8]

As with the island shopping and African safaris, it was just something fun to do at the time, but with bugs, bad food, and humidity. It wasn't a yacht or Hilton Hotel. Besides, their guru had an eye for Western women. A bookkeeper and a fleet of Rolls-Royces, too. Not the best example to follow.

When the Maharishi allegedly made a sexual advance toward actress Mia Farrow, the Beatles became disillusioned. Lennon even wrote a cleverly disguised song about the experience for *The White Album*, titled "Sexy Sadie." He admitted, "That was inspired by Maharishi. I wrote it when we had our bags packed and were leaving. It was the last piece I wrote before I left India. I just called him 'Sexy Sadie' instead of 'Maharishi, what have you done? You made a fool of everyone . . . ' I was just using the situation to write a song, rather calculatingly but also to express what I felt. I was leaving the Maharishi with a bad taste. You know, it seems that my partings are always not as nice as I'd like them to be."[9]

Lennon told *Rolling Stone* that when the Maharishi asked why he was leaving, he replied, "Well, if you're so cosmic, you'll know why!"[10]

Harrison didn't leave everything back in India. Nor was it a total bust. He was still intrigued by Eastern philosophy, specifically a swami who practiced the worship of the Indian god Krishna. The swami, Srila Prabhupada, started out preaching in New York City parks to hippies and more strait-laced youth alike. His movement expanded a year later by relocating to San Francisco at the height of the intersection of Haight and Ashbury Streets.

When it reached England, it caught Harrison's attention. He bankrolled the swami. His star power and checkbook ended up putting the Krishnas front and center. Harrison even recorded "Hare Krishna Mantra," which was a top-selling single around the world (except in the United States). More than a dozen Krishna devotees and their children moved into Harrison's Friar Park mansion, cooking vegetarian meals, chanting day and night, and leaving inspirational messages each morning on his kitchen chalkboard.

Chris O'Dell, who worked for Apple Records and lived with George and Pattie Harrison at the time, said the Krishnas were nice people but eventually wore out their welcome. Washing machines were full of diapers. The cleaning ladies complained that the Krishna wing of the house was a mess and reeked of saffron. Dishes piled up in the sink, candle wax dripped everywhere, and their kids ran wild.

"The little sayings on the blackboard, often taken from the *Bhagavad Gita*, the sacred Hindu scriptures, began to piss us off," O'Dell said. "We interpreted them as preachy little quotes intended to chide us for our profligate ways or undisguised attempts to convert us."[11]

Visible fissures also began to appear in the Beatles' façade, which would eventually lead to their 1970 breakup. Any spiritual enlightenment from then on was pursued individually. Harrison continued his path with the Krishnas.

After Lennon's controversial statement that the Beatles were more popular than Jesus, he traveled a convoluted path with Christianity, Buddhism, agnosticism, and the occult, often condemning organized religion in interviews. For all his banter, he always acknowledged Jesus's existence, but remained highly skeptical. (More on that and his tragic death in a later chapter).

Starr, who went through a two-decade period of heavy drinking, finally got sober in 1988. He entered a treatment center in Tucson, Arizona, for six weeks of rehab and detox. He later leaned on God through Alcoholics Anonymous.

"Being out on this quest for a long time, it's all about finding yourself," Starr told one newspaper outlet. "For me, God is in my life. I don't hide from that. I think the search has been on since the '60s. I stepped off the path for many years and found my way (back) onto it, thank God."[12]

McCartney was less specific. He said in 2012 he has a "personal faith in something good, but it doesn't really go much further than that."[13] In another interview, he said, "I believe in a spirit, that's the best I can put it. I think there's something greater than us, and I love it; I'm grateful to it, but just like everyone else on the planet, I can't pin it down . . . I'm happy not pinning it down. So, I pick bits out of all the religions. I like many things that Buddhists say. I like a lot of things that Jesus said, that Mohammad said." He concludes, "Be cool and you'll be all right. That's Rock and Roll religion."

Paul said he still speaks to George Harrison's spirit through a large fir tree on his East Sussex estate in England, a gift from "The Quiet Beatle" prior to his 2001 death from lung cancer.

"George was very into horticulture, a really good gardener," McCartney told NPR host Mary Louise Kelley in December 2020. "So, he gave me a tree as a present. It's a big fir tree, and it's by my gate. As I was leaving my house this morning, I get out of the car, close the gate, and look up at the tree and say, 'Hi, George.' There he is, growing strongly."[14]

I had the opportunity to meet George Harrison in Hawaii many years ago.

We were staying in Hana, where Harrison owned a home. I was sitting on the beach when who comes up and sits right behind me but the former Beatle himself. He spoke with that unmistakable Liverpudlian accent, and I finally mustered up the courage to engage him in conversation. Being a hardcore Beatles fan, I must admit, I was seriously starstruck. Harrison was not a very approachable person. He had already completed his first Traveling Wilburys album with his friends Bob Dylan, Roy Orbison, Tom Petty, and Jeff Lynne. I told him how I loved the collaborative quality of the music. He replied that I would like the next one even more. Funny thing is, when I mentioned the Beatles, he went dead silent. When I talked about the Wilburys, he lit up. There was a period when Harrison simply did not want to discuss being a part of the most famous and influential band in music history. McCartney went through that phase as well.

It's understandable. He, along with the others, was in the eye of the hurricane, but they had only each other to hold on to. Harrison once said in an interview, "(The fans) gave their money, and they gave their screams. But the Beatles kind of gave their nervous systems. They used us as an excuse to go mad, the world did, and then blamed it on us."

George Harrison's intensive path with the Krishnas ended with a pilgrimage to Benares, India, in 2001, where he bathed in the Ganges River to prepare for his death. Since the late 1990s, he had been fighting a long and hard battle with lung cancer and was losing.

In an unfortunate incident that illustrates how Harrison could not escape the long shadow of the Beatles, the doctor who was treating him brought his children to a Staten Island home where Harrison was undergoing stereotactic radiosurgery treatment. Breaking protocol, he took them into the room where

Harrison was bedridden and in great discomfort, and had George listen to his son play the guitar. Afterward, the doctor took the guitar, put it in Harrison's lap, and asked him to sign it. Harrison resisted, telling the doctor, "I do not even know if I can spell my name anymore." The doctor, unwilling to take no for an answer, took hold of George's hand and guided the ex-Beatle through his autograph.[15]

After exhausting all his medical options, Harrison decided he did not want to wither away in a hospital and flew in a private jet to Los Angeles, where he spent his final days in a Beverly Hills home owned by Paul McCartney. While glucose drip-fed intravenously into Harrison's body, his wife, Olivia, and son, Dhani, kept vigil. Ravi Shankar was also present, gently playing his sitar. Two friends from the Krishna faith chanted quietly into their meditation beads while a Hare Krishna priest read from the *Bhagavad Gita*. Framed photos of Hindu gods Krishna and Rama sat on a bedside table, practically staring at Harrison when he passed away at 1:20 p.m. on November 29, 2001. He was fifty-eight years old. George Harrison's ashes were scattered in the Ganges River three months after his passing.

Harrison was a searcher throughout his life, understanding that the answer was not in the fame, money, power, drugs, or lifestyle of a top-tier rock star.

In "All Those Years Ago," his 1981 tribute song to his mate and fellow Beatle, John Lennon, George also sang of God, mankind, and the reason for our existence.

The Beatles' spiritual journey is not a clean or simple story. It's actually rather confusing. Each of them came to vastly different conclusions about what enlightenment meant to them. They traveled different paths and made different choices. But George had it right when he said of God, "He's the only reason we exist."

These pied pipers led a generation down a long and winding road—and sadly, for the most part, it was the blind leading the blind.

CHAPTER THREE

27 Club

There's a famously macabre gang nobody planned to join. It's called the 27 Club.

It's composed of rock stars and musicians who tragically —incredibly—died at age twenty-seven. The causes were usually from some type of excess: alcohol or drug abuse or death by misadventure. Sadly, the club has continued to add to its numbers over the years.

Its earliest members were four rock legends: Brian Jones of the Rolling Stones, Jimi Hendrix, Janis Joplin, and Jim Morrison of the Doors. They all died within two years of each other. Joplin and Hendrix died within weeks of each other in 1970.

That was a pivotal year for me. Not only was it the year the Beatles broke up—it was the year I came into a relationship with God through Jesus Christ. It was truly the dawning of a new age for me.

As teens and young adults, we looked up to these rock stars. They were more influential to us than our teachers, our political leaders, and in some instances, even our parents. Their music, lives, fashion, and attitudes voiced everything we felt at the time. We copied almost everything they did, including their drug habits. I had already seen the effects of drugs in my own life, so it was not a surprise to see them claim the lives of my rock idols. It changed me, too. I went from a fun-loving, wise-cracking, creative young man to basically being a doper. In school, my grades plummeted, and my motivation to do anything meaningful crashed and burned. I just wanted to get high pretty much all the time and do nothing else. Even before I became a Christian, I came to my senses and got off that path, seeing it for the deception it was.

When I came to faith in 1970, the Beatles' last single, "The Long and Winding Road" dominated the radio airwaves. It was a Paul McCartney-penned-tune that resonated with me. In it, he sings, "Don't keep me waiting here. Lead me to your door." Even as a teenager, I was ready for a change in my life, because my long and winding road had led nowhere. Though I was only seventeen, I felt as though I were seventy. I had lived through my mother's wild ride of seven husbands, lots of boyfriends in between, and out-of-control alcoholism. These were white-knuckle years that aged me internally. It sent me on a search. Turned out, I was following the wrong people. The rock stars I put so much stock in were essentially lost souls and didn't know any more than I did.

Some of them joined the 27 Club.

Sadly, these artists never got the chance to continue their life's work or to find the peace they longed for in their hearts. This mostly stemmed from difficult childhoods and feeling like outsiders.

Jimi Hendrix, in my humble opinion, was the greatest guitar player who ever lived. I was a huge fan of his music and owned several of his albums, which I played constantly on my turntable. What he did with that instrument—playing behind his head, playing with his teeth, getting sounds out of it no one thought possible at the time—set him apart. When he lit his guitar on fire at the 1969 Newport Pop Festival, the act was without precedent.

Hendrix was the product of a broken and dysfunctional home. Both of his parents were alcoholics who continually lived in poverty. His mother, Lucille Jeter, was a teenager when she had him. His dad, Al Hendrix, had a long history of alcoholism. Young Jimi's home life was fractured and unhappy. He had four brothers who were given away or taken away by the state and placed into foster care. The brothers would not be reunited for several years.

Hendrix's mother died of liver cirrhosis when he was just sixteen, leaving him emotionally bereft. As a result, he was soft-spoken and introverted. And he had an ear for music. While helping his dad at work, cleaning someone's house, he found a damaged ukulele with only one string in a pile of junk to be tossed out. The teenaged Hendrix learned to play well with just one string, mimicking songs he'd heard on the radio, including Elvis Presley's "Hound Dog."

A decade later, Hendrix singlehandedly redefined the sonic and music vocabulary of the electric guitar and rocketed to stardom with psychedelic anthems such as "Purple Haze" and "Foxy Lady." He gave perhaps the most legendary and memorable performance of the decade at Woodstock in 1969.

An often-overlooked fact is that Hendrix served in the military. Before he turned nineteen, he was busted twice for riding in stolen cars. So when he was given a choice between prison or the army, he chose the latter. His rendition of "The Star-Spangled Banner" at Woodstock sprang from a man who knew what it meant to serve his country. Al Aronowitz of the *New York Post* later wrote, "It was the most electrifying moment of Woodstock, and it was probably the single greatest moment of the sixties."[1]

Hendrix died on September 18, 1970, in London. He had spent the previous night drinking and smoking hash with his German girlfriend, Monika Dannemann. The autopsy report stated he asphyxiated on his own vomit after taking too many sleeping pills (he suffered from chronic insomnia). The coroner estimated Hendrix took as many as nine tablets that fateful night, and determined it was mostly likely an accident. What a tragic loss of such a talented man with so much to offer the world musically.

We don't know how Hendrix felt about God or if he subscribed to a particular faith, but he did once say, "We call our music 'electric church music.' Because it's like a religion to us."[2] All these years later, I wish Jesus could have been included in that statement.

· · ·

There is no mystery about where Janis Joplin, who joined the 27 Club three weeks after Hendrix, stood when it came to her faith. The rebellious and self-destructive Texan found her voice in the church choir (and later got kicked out, according to her sister). Joplin's short but impactful career inspired countless other performers, including Joan Jett, Alicia Keys, and Pink. But growing up in Port Arthur, Texas, she was a misfit and an outcast, and thus retreated into her own private world.

Joplin was a free spirit whose tendency toward rebellion got her into a lot of trouble. She caught grief from her high school classmates for the way she dressed and for her early belief in racial desegregation, which was linked to her love of the blues—particularly the music of Billie Holiday and Bessie Smith. For that, she was called a "pig" and was mercilessly bullied by her male classmates, who threw pennies at her and even groped her in the hallways. She longed for acceptance, but said her schoolmates laughed her "out of class, out of town, and out of the state, man."[3] College was an equally terrible experience.

She embraced hippie culture and gave drug- and alcohol-fueled performances, often swigging straight from a bottle of Southern Comfort at gigs. But Joplin also had a very sensitive side—she loved painting, poetry, and literature. The two sides of her nature inevitably clashed, and substance abuse was a natural coping mechanism. The wild child artist was a tortured soul. Sadly, it's this very combination that makes great artists so impactful.

Introduced first as the lead singer of Big Brother and the Holding Company and later breaking out as a solo artist, Joplin became America's first female rock star after her stellar performance at the 1967 Monterey International Pop Festival. She also dove headfirst into the rock star lifestyle, sinking into a hunger for alcohol, narcotics, and anything bad for her body and soul. She tried many times to get clean, but always relapsed.

On the early morning of October 4, 1970, a lifetime of excess caught up with the "Queen of Rock 'n Roll." Joplin died after taking a rogue batch of heroin, overdosing while recording an unfinished album that was released three months after her death. It was the classic *Pearl*, which featured her No. 1 single "Me and Bobby McGee" (written by Kris Kristofferson).

Janis Joplin's life—which held so much promise—was cut short with a tragic ending, sending her straight into the unfortunate 27 Club.

• • •

Biographers have often described Jim Morrison as a dutiful and highly intelligent child, excelling at school in his early years. He was particularly gifted in reading, writing, and drawing, which later bore out in his art. He grew up in a two-parent household and did not have to deal with the pains of poverty like Hendrix, nor was he a social outcast like Joplin. In fact, he was president of his fifth-grade class and made the honor roll with little or no effort.

His father, George Morrison, was a naval aviator who quickly rose to the rank of general. Being in the military meant being on the move. By age four, "Jimmy" had lived in five different places along both coasts of the U.S. Since his father was gone for long periods, his mother, Clara, became the disciplinarian. Jimmy grew rebellious. It's a common refrain for military brats: the father, accustomed to thousands of men obeying his every command, comes home to a child who is unruly and insubordinate. They clash, they fight, they grow distant from one another. Those negative feelings must be placed somewhere.

According to people who grew up with him, Morrison started showing up at school drunk at the age of twelve or thirteen. His illicit drug use began in earnest during his years at UCLA; he began experimenting with just about any drug he could secure, seeking the next "experience" and often running off into the desert for days on end, dropping acid and hallucinating.

Morrison first met Ray Manzarek at a coffee shop on the UCLA campus, but the two didn't really bond until they saw each other at Venice Beach in July 1965. Manzarek was sitting on the sand, meditating, when Morrison spotted him and re-introduced himself. Manzarek asked what he was up to; Morrison told him he was living at the beach with a friend and writing songs. Manzarek asked to hear one. Morrison sang, "Moonlight Drive." Manzarek said, "Far out, let's make a million dollars." And the Doors were born.

When "Light My Fire" was released in 1967, Morrison became a bona fide rock icon. With his tight leather pants and hypnotic performances, he also became a sex symbol to the young girls of the 1960s. (I have heard stories about a fourteen-year-old girl named Catherine Martin who went to hear the band in person and swooned over Morrison like so many others. Seven years later, Cathe Martin officially became Cathe Laurie, and she has been my wife since 1974.)

I remember "Light My Fire" being so popular that, while walking on the beach, I could hear that song on nearly everyone's transistor radio. (Yes, that's how we listened on the go back then.) The Doors instantly became famous after the song was released, and Morrison demonstrated he couldn't handle that notoriety. Not one bit. He was a superstar at war with his own demons, and he abused alcohol and a variety of drugs. His behavior caused problems.

According to bandmate Robby Krieger: "It was always a bummer. We had this group which we all knew had the potential to be something really big, and Jim was trying to sabotage it by messing up at every turn. We would schedule a rehearsal, Jim wouldn't show, and we'd get a call from Blythe, Arizona, telling us that he was in jail."[4]

A few years later, he tried to shake the madness of rock star life, as well as his addiction to drugs and alcohol. Excessive beer drinking had bloated Morrison's once-chiseled face and lean body. He moved to Paris, France, with his longtime girlfriend Pamela Courson (who, ironically, also died at age twenty-seven) to focus on his poetry and live his life out of the public spotlight for a while.

Morrison's premature death in Paris remains obscured by mystery, rumor, and conspiracy theories of a coverup concerning its actual cause (and even location). The death certificate stated he died of heart failure, but no autopsy was ever performed. It's believed that Morrison's body, which Courson found submerged in the bathtub around 6:00 a.m. on July 3, 1971, remained there until the undertakers finally arrived with a body bag seventy-two hours later.

The rock star and iconoclast believed and dabbled in a lot of things, even participating in a solemn Celtic wedding ceremony called "handfasting" with journalist Patricia Kennealy in June 1970. Friends say it didn't mean much to him; he took part in it because it was exciting and taboo.

But there was another side to Jim Morrison—a more thoughtful and considerate side. A priest by the name of Fred L. Stiegemeier approached the singer at a soundcheck before a Doors concert in the late 1960s, wanting to know Morrison's belief system. The meeting was caught on camera for a documentary called *Feast of Friends*, which features Morrison presenting Doors concerts as Dionysian rituals, resulting in a sort of collective ecstasy where the divine transcends the mundane and the ego is subverted to the primal unconscious mind. In reality, they were simply concerts; but Morrison saw them differently.

Wearing a black suit and white clerical collar, puffing calmly on a pipe, Stiegemeier gently buttonholed Morrison as he stood with the rest of the band on a very noisy stage. He asked to speak with Morrison privately.

"I don't know if you know the experience of the disciples fifty days after the resurrection," Stiegemeier said. "They had been left alone by The Man and He told them to stay in Jerusalem until something happens. The event that happened was intense communication—not only communication within their little circle, but communication with everyone that heard them. I think this is perhaps related, in a sense."

"I can try and explain anything," Morrison said respectfully. The Lizard King who snarled from the stage was not present. This was a thoughtful young man, open to being engaged and questioned. "We try to provoke sort of a religious experience."

"This is what I really appreciate," Stiegemeier replied.

"In a sense, it's a lot of people communicating in one room," Morrison said. "It's 50 percent physical. The records are only half of it, really. There's a whole other element."

"It strikes me as a tremendous mystique about what you're involved in here," Stiegemeier said. "It's much more than anything on the surface. Most of the 'establishment,' they're really concerned about what the hell you're pulling off, and it's suspect."

"This kind of thing has been going on for a long time," Morrison said. "It's kind of like secular religion in a way, I guess."

Stiegemeier asked how he could reach Morrison, and they exchanged mailing addresses. The priest thanked the rock star and added, "Just don't tell my bishop."[5]

I wish this priest had simply told the searching Jim Morrison that there was a God in Heaven who loved him and would transform his life if he gave Him a chance. I also wish someone could have told that to the other 27 Club members.

Morrison was obsessed with death his entire life. He famously sang about breaking through to the "other side" and Indians scattered on a dawn's bleeding highway—words he penned about his family allegedly coming across a car accident in the New Mexico desert when he was a kid.[6] Guitarist Robby Krieger referred to Morrison's frequent suicidal, downer moods. No one was ever going to mistake Morrison for a member of the duo who wrote "Love Me Do."

In any event, his cause of death remains a mystery to this day. As I said, French authorities simply pegged the cause as heart failure and left it at that. Fans still gather at his grave in Paris to pay homage to their hero. What a tragic ending for such a talented man.

• • •

Tragically, new members have been joining the 27 Club since then. In 1994, Kurt Cobain, lead singer of Nirvana, the biggest grunge band of all time, died from a self-inflicted shotgun wound to the head. He was missing for six days before his body was discovered; his mother, Wendy O'Connor, had a premonition he was dead. And for good reason: he had overdosed a month before from a combination of champagne and Rohypnol. In the aftermath of his death, O'Connor told a reporter, "Now he's gone and joined that stupid club. I told him not to join that stupid club."[7]

Cobain's parents were divorced, and he split his time between them as a child. When he became too much to handle, they would send him to live with friends. At one point, this included a born-again Christian family. He joined the church and attended services, but he later vehemently denounced Christianity and turned toward Buddhism.

• • •

Meanwhile, British chanteuse Amy Winehouse was raised Jewish. Although she was proud of her heritage, she was not religious at all. "Being Jewish to me is about being together as a real family. It's not about lighting candles and saying a berakah," she said in an interview.[8]

Fresh-faced, full of talent and energy, she worked hard to be heard. Winehouse was a talented singer-songwriter who played her own guitar. She even recorded a duet with her musical hero, Tony Bennett, who said of her, "Some people think that anyone could sing jazz, but they can't. It's a gift of learning how to syncopate, but it's also a spirit that you're either born with or you're not. And Amy was born with that spirit."[9]

As she became a global success, Winehouse took every kind of drug in existence, but her real drug of choice was alcohol. In 2011, she died of accidental alcohol poisoning. Everybody seemed to know it was coming but couldn't do much for her. She longed for success and fame, and finally found it to be . . . empty.

"Fame is like terminal cancer," she said. "I wouldn't wish it on anyone."[10]

These people had mishmashes of beliefs, and some had none at all. They were in constant turmoil and pain, and fought to get out of that headspace. The cycle of addiction and dealing with the complexities of fame was overwhelming. They were busy negotiating their new reality: losing their sense of self, determining who was really their friend, cracking the whip because their career was constantly on the line, and trying to keep their place on the mountaintop.

For people that young, everything can seem hopeless or heavy or serious; someone older would be more capable of pulling out of it or realizing things aren't as dire as they seem. I remember thinking it was the end of the world when stuff happened to me at that age, whereas now I'd just shake my head and deal with it. It's been said that your personal growth screeches to a sudden stop the minute you become famous. Over time, celebrities become overprotected and pampered, which can lead to difficulties in learning how to attend to everyday tasks such as driving a car, doing laundry, cooking meals, or scheduling a doctor's appointment. I once heard of an NBA star who suffered from a bad cold for weeks because he had no idea how to contact a doctor.

Socializing with normal peers also can be awkward. Celebrities exposed to the fast-paced world of show business often leave their old friends in the dust. It's hard to sit down with Joey from the neighborhood and sympathize with how Mikey is having a tough time in school, how Joanie's getting laid off from the clinic, and how they just might be able to afford a week at the shore this summer when you're driving home from the studio in the wee hours of the morning in a knee-high Italian car (which you didn't really want, but you had no idea what else to do with the money) to eat something your fitness trainer put on your diet which was measured by your nutritionist before being cooked by your private chef. You're not a normal person anymore, and associating with normal people is like trying to talk to a bear or an alien. (And vice versa: Joey has no idea what it's like to kill an hour in the green room with two other bold-faced names or to hire a good estate manager to take care of the house in London.) Contrary to popular belief, adversity is not the greatest test of character; overnight success is.

Just ask Dez Dickerson, who was Prince's dazzling lead guitarist from 1978 to 1983.

"(Fame) was like this vertical takeoff, and suddenly there are more people around you. 'Oh, we have roadies now?' 'Oh, we have bodyguards now?' And they're there for a reason, too. We experienced mini riots; we couldn't walk down the street, and they had to cordon off the floor of our hotel," Dickerson said. "What that does to your head is beyond description, and what it does to the human psyche is a whole other thing. There's this internal mechanism that unconsciously begins to take form, and your equilibrium gets so skewed that you find yourself doing and saying things that aren't you. You become your own press release. It's difficult to articulate if you haven't experienced it."[11]

• • •

It goes without saying that twenty-seven is an age when most people feel themselves to be ten feet tall and bulletproof. But when you're a rock star, a drink, a puff, a snort, or an injection can't possibly do any harm—not when you're on top of the world. Right?

Drug use among both the famous and unfamous alike in the 1960s is well-documented. What many people don't realize now is that by the 1970s, it wasn't just the hippies using anymore. It was everyone. Pot and coke had claimed beachheads at the country club, albeit in the bathroom and on the golf course after dark. The chic were hoovering up Bolivian marching powder on the way out to nightclubs and discos. Hollywood accountants kept two sets of books: above the line and below the line. If Woody Allen was doing it in *Annie Hall*, you can bet countless others had their nose to the mirror, too.

Heavy drinking was acceptable to everyone. The three-martini lunch was a perfectly normal way to close business deals (in three-piece suits, of course). Grandparents made pitchers of Bloody Mary on Sunday mornings and sipped martinis on week-nights during conversations that usually began, "During the war we . . ." A hangover was a sign of accomplishment. Bars opened at 6:00 a.m. so the tradeworkers could come in for a shot and a beer with a raw egg in it before heading to the job site. The bar cars on commuter trains were absolutely packed every night, the floor slick with beer and the air blue with smoke. And no one really cared. Keith Richards famously posed in front of a sign which read "A Drug Free America Comes First," during the Rolling Stones' 1972 *STP* tour, to the side-splitting laughter of everyone under thirty.

We've discovered over time that abuses can and do have an accumulative effect on the body. The Stooges founding bass player Dave "Zander" Alexander, also twenty-seven, drank so much that he developed pancreatitis. One night in February 1975, his lungs filled with fluid, and he died of pulmonary edema.

Rolling Stones founder and rhythm guitarist Brian Jones's excesses had a debilitative effect on his physical and mental health. He was difficult, unfriendly, antisocial and, at the end of his stint with the Stones in the late 1960s, usually inebriated or high. His contributions to the group diminished greatly. On July 3, 1969, a month after he was fired from the group, he drowned in the pool of his home in Sussex, England. An autopsy report showed his heart was fat and flabby, and his liver was twice the normal weight. Alcohol was also in his system (the equivalent of three pints of beer). "Brian was one huge gaping crybaby all the time: 'help me, talk to me, love me.' Then people would try to do that, and he'd change," said Jo Bergman, the Stones' personal assistant from 1967 to 1973. "It was very rough. He was six years old all the time . . . How do you give psychiatric help to a Rolling Stone?"

I'm sure it's hard for the public to accept that celebrities have it tough in their spacious mansions, sports cars, and the jets-and-limousine world they inhabit after they've hit it big, but that's only what you see on the outside. Humor me for a second and consider what these folks must deal with internally. Once someone becomes famous, he instantly loses ownership of his life and personal freedom. I don't care what era it is—that's a difficult transition for anyone.

Recently, another name was "honorarily" added to the 27 Club. I'm talking about Avicii.

Tim Bergling, a Swedish DJ who adopted the stage name Avicii when he launched his career at the age of sixteen, was at the forefront of electronic dance music (EDM) and enjoying a measure of success few will ever experience. Massive crowds showed up to watch him perform at venues across the globe. Arenas were full of people singing his songs and chanting his name repeatedly. Behind the scenes however, Avicii was exhausted. He drank heavily as he watched his life unraveling all around him. Feeling like he had reached his limit, he told his managers if he continued touring, it would ultimately lead to his death.

Throughout his short life, Avicii dealt with several health issues, including acute pancreatitis that was a byproduct of his excessive drinking. Yet, the tours continued to be booked, and he maintained a brutal travel schedule that took him across the world. Predictably, he continued to go downhill even as he found himself longing for more. Deep down inside, he just wanted to find some peace.

Avicii made it to the age of twenty-eight, but only by seven months. He was depleted from the endless touring and decided to retire to a beach in Madagascar. While on vacation in the Middle East in 2018, he took his own life by cutting himself with a broken wine bottle.

His family released a statement in the aftermath of his death: "He really struggled with thoughts about meaning, life, and happiness. He could not go on any longer. He wanted to find peace."[12]

I wish I could have met with this guy and talked about the very things he longed for: meaning, life, and happiness. The fact is, we all long for those things. You could say we are hard-wired to seek them. This is nothing new.

Honestly, I wish I could have had conversations with these rock and pop icons of the past. I would have told them that drugs were not the answer. Nor was fame, unhinged promiscuity, or any of the other trappings that go with a rock star life.

I would have told them that their talent was given to them by God, and that He had an amazing, fulfilling plan for them. I would have told them that if Christ came into their hearts, He would fill the void they were trying to fill with all the cheap substitutes this culture offers. I would have told them their lives mattered greatly, and they were loved and needed.

I can't go back in time and say that to Jimi, Jim, Janis, Kurt, Amy, Brian, or Tim.

But I *am* saying it to you right now.

CHAPTER FOUR

Jesus Christ Superstar

Rarely do popular culture and Christianity intersect, but it happened in the early 1970s in what was considered America's last Great Awakening.

The Great Awakenings were a series of periods of religious revival. The first happened in colonial times before the American Revolution. The second one (1795–1835) not only brought a greater sense of religious identity but also raised issues of reform, including temperance, abolition, and women's rights. The third Great Awakening took place between the 1850s and early 1900s, primarily in New York City, and it started as a simple prayer meeting led by an ordinary man named Jeremiah Lanphier. Each of these revivals brought people to faith and dramatically impacted the culture.

I lived through and witnessed firsthand the most recent Great Awakening—you could even say I'm a product of it. The Jesus Movement started as a groundswell in Southern California before spreading nationwide. Plays, movies, and songs got their moment in the spotlight in the late 1960s and early 1970s, giving Jesus superstar status among youth and the pop culture elite—some for better, some for worse. But one of the most significant aspects of this movement is that it was being led by young people, which may have been a first among spiritual awakenings. Many of these kids, including me, came to faith because we had followed classic rock musicians like the Beatles down the primrose path of promise only to find ourselves in the Pit of Despair.

My life was transformed by Jesus after a long struggle with drugs and drinking. I had lost my way. But soon, I found the answer: a relationship with God through His son, Jesus Christ. So simple, yet so amazing.

Many believe this movement began with a singer named Larry Norman. To be clear, he was not the first person to play rock with a Christian message, but he is regarded by many as the father of Contemporary Christian rock. The talented Texan was also a songwriter, record producer, and label owner. He had the looks, he had the skill, he had the charisma—and he had the inner conflict that haunts many accomplished artists.

He was sometimes unfriendly to fans, outright hostile to record executives, and even hurtful to many of those who loved and worked with him. But his music was mesmerizing. He was supremely gifted, and his admirers included the likes of Bob Dylan, Cliff Richard, and Bono. Norman sold out venues including London's Royal Albert Hall, the Hollywood Palladium, and the Sydney Opera House in Australia. He played at the White House. Former Vice President Mike Pence once told me he had dedicated his life to Christ at a 1978 music festival headlined by Norman. Even Paul McCartney recognized Norman's star potential, apparently telling him, "You could be famous if you'd just drop the God stuff."[1]

Norman's flower power band People! charted many regional singles, had a million-seller in the 1968 release "I Love You," and opened for or shared the bill with acts like Van Morrison, the Animals, the Doors, the Who, Janis Joplin, and Jimi Hendrix. After his gig with People! ended in mid-1968, Norman worked as an in-house writer for Capitol Records, the most prestigious music label of the era, where he penned songs, musicals, and rock operas during the day and preached on the street to businessmen, transvestites, prostitutes, and hippies at night.

He was an unusual artist because, by his own testimony, he did not compose songs for the church; he wrote pop and rock songs with a message about faith for unbelievers. These weren't kumbaya songs, either. They were gritty and real. For instance, his lyrics from "Why Don't You Look into Jesus" talked about sipping whiskey from a paper cup and drowning your sorrows until you can't stand up.

Norman wrote about what he knew and witnessed as a human, musician, and street poet: venereal disease, shooting heroin, infidelity, and the side of life that no one liked to talk about. You were never going to hear any of this stuff in the church basement. His status as a Christian outsider was culturally relevant and provocative.

His 1969 album *Upon This Rock* was a lot of things. It was considered the first true Contemporary Christian rock album, and according to one critic, the *Sgt. Pepper's* of the genre. I know I felt the same way when I first heard it a few months after its release.

At the time, I was a long-haired high school senior at Newport Beach's Harbor High and a newly minted Christian. At seventeen, I was willing to stop listening to rock and roll if I could find faith-based music that was equivalent to what I had been reared on—the timeless rock of the 1960s.

I finally found what I was looking for inside a local coffee shop. (Well, it wasn't really a coffee shop, but they had coffee there.)

It was a place where we would gather for prayer, and then we would go out and share the Gospel. There was a record player, and one day I was flipping through what really looked like the lamest albums of all time and going, "Bad, bad, bad, bad." As a seventeen-year-old, the artists appeared to me to be dorky-looking people trying to look cool, which is the most uncool thing you possibly could do. Then I came across a record called *Upon This Rock*. On the cover, Larry Norman is shown with long blond hair and his arms are stretched out, reaching for something.

What is this? I thought.

I plopped the platter down on the turntable and proceeded to be blown away. Great lyrics, catchy melody, and it was even humorous at times. To me, that was the first real record of what we would later call "Jesus Music." Album sales for *Upon This Rock* were a disaster, but it jumpstarted an entire genre.

Record executives weren't even aware they had a Christian album on their hands. Norman was employed at Capitol Records as a rock writer, but he never stopped by to meet or schmooze executives in marketing and promotion, and he didn't have a manager who would go to bat for him, either. The album was still a landmark work because it was the first to prove that rock could be Christian and popular . . . and good.

Norman's popularity extended throughout the 1970s, but in time his fame—like everyone else's—waned. By the late 1980s, he was a "legacy artist" who no longer opened big festivals or had a lucrative record contract with a major label. He was getting by on his name only, and even that was thinning. That was right around the new millennium, and about the time I met him.

I was speaking at a huge Christian music festival when I, by chance, happened upon Larry, sitting by himself on a worn couch behind the massive stage. He still had the trademark long hair and, at that time, he also sported a scraggly beard.

Artists and roadies walked back and forth in front of him, none seeming to take any notice of him at all. I took a seat next to him, introduced myself, and told him how his first record had impacted me. His eyes lit up. I then said, gesturing toward the concert stage, "Larry, none of this would be happening today if you had not picked up your guitar and written songs that changed lives. You were the forerunner of it all, and I thank you for it!" He smiled, and he knew I meant every word. Larry Norman was a true living legend and did not receive the accolades he deserved in his lifetime.

In his later years, Norman's albums became less and less compelling because he was releasing them just to pay steep medical bills. The final years of his life were marked by frequent stays in the hospital for serious heart problems. He died at the age of sixty in 2008.

Today, critics agree that Larry Norman is to Christian music what Bob Dylan is to modern music. But Norman's legacy never faded away or dimmed—quite the opposite. It took off and went in directions even he couldn't imagine.

In the late 1960s and early 1970s, the Byrds, George Harrison, Jackson Browne, Edwin Hawkins Singers, Pacific Gas & Electric, Yvonne Elliman, Ocean, the Doobie Brothers, Glen Campbell, and Anne Murray all sang about God in different ways. Their songs were big hits and popular on the radio, and it was clear there was a spiritual theme to them from "Jesus Is Just Alright" to "Oh, Happy Day." Others, like "Spirit in The Sky" by Norman Greenbaum and "My Sweet Lord" by George Harrison (where he sings of both Jesus and Krishna), were muddled in their message.

The next landmark moment came in the last place anyone would expect.

. . .

It involved a balding, married, middle-aged father of four—a preacher who presided over a failing church—and a truly spacey hippie with an Old Testament beard and a new rap. The combination of these two people who had nothing in common in terms of personality, life experience, background, or appearance—Chuck Smith and Lonnie Frisbee—was the spiritual equivalent of The Odd Couple; but together they were dynamite . . . for a time.

Smith was the missionary to a tribe that had been ignored by the church. Frisbee was its Pied Piper, drawing them into Smith's Calvary Chapel in Costa Mesa, California in such numbers that services spilled over into a tent. There was no legalism, dress codes, or heavy guilt trips at these services. Calvary Chapel preached the love of God and forgiveness through the blood of Christ. That resonated with the new congregants. Crowds got so big that the county sent a fire marshal to keep the youths from blocking the aisle. (The fire marshal ended up getting saved during the altar call at the end of the service.)

These weren't your typical churchgoers. Forget suits, ties, and dresses. Sunday best for these faithful was embroidered jeans, headbands, beads, feathers, and granny glasses. Some of the bare-foot faithful poked their toes through the communion cupholders on the backs of the pews. Others sat cross-legged in the aisles. No one had ever seen anything like this in church before, and Chuck Smith's older congregants sat wide-eyed, their mouths agape.

Chuck and Kay Smith began inviting people to stay in their home. At one point, they shoehorned thirty-five people into their two-bedroom house, having built bunks in the garage to accommodate them all. Kids crashed on every available spot on the floor; one even slept in their bathtub. The Smiths also baptized their houseguests in their small backyard swimming pool. In May 1968, they rented a second home in Costa Mesa as a Christian communal crash pad for hippies, known as "The House of Miracles." When they outgrew that space, a realtor they knew offered a nine-unit motel that he owned in Newport Beach for use as another Christian commune. A half-dozen more of these communal homes sprouted up over the course of the following year.

If Smith's older congregants' eyes widened like saucers at the sight of all this, their ears were under an even bigger assault.

Not only did the Jesus freaks eschew traditional church attire, they shed any affection for traditional church music as well. For this generation, music was everything. Great music was everywhere—the Beatles, Buffalo Springfield, the Byrds, the Beach Boys, the Rolling Stones, the Who, Eric Clapton, Jimi Hendrix, Motown, and the great sounds of surf and folk rock from Southern California. Music was bigger than sporting events, and the industry outpaced the movie business. So far, this music had dominated almost every part of the culture and entertainment world—but it had not yet penetrated the church.

But that was about to change.

That transformation occurred when a few musicians who had been saved at Calvary offered to play a few songs at a service. They played a sample song for Chuck Smith. He was hesitant at first, but after hearing the lyrics and the group singing with such conviction, he willingly caved and asked them to play at a Saturday night service. The group was elated, but there was one small hitch: one band member was spending the weekend in the county jail for a pot conviction. If he could get bailed out, it would be a heavenly service, man. Through the grace of God and a talented bail bondsman, the musician made it to the service that evening, and the place exploded.

That group, Love Song, was the first mainstream Christian rock band. They were considered the "Beatles of Jesus Rock." It wasn't what the band did that was so special, but rather, where and when they were doing it. No one had ever seen guitars and drums in a church before. The music sounded like rock, but instead of saying "rebel," it said "be joyful, be saved, and come to Christ." Contemporary Christian music was about to launch. It was a special moment in time.

Six months later, at least a dozen new Christian acts with names like Mustard Seed Faith, Blessed Hope, Joy, Country Faith, and Children of the Day followed Love Song. The Way, a band that sounded a lot like the pop group America, racked up quite a few Christian hits in its heyday.

I was privileged to have a front-row seat and got to know a lot of these musicians personally; I really admired their talent. I was doing graphic design at the time and did the art for several Christian records from that era, including the Sweet Comfort Band. These acts would show up regularly at one of Calvary Chapel's mid-week services with fresh songs that we would all learn and sing in short order.

When I first began attending Calvary Chapel, the place was packed wall-to-wall with people sitting in the pews and on the green shag-carpeted floor. We swayed in unison to the melody of songs like "Thy Loving Kindness" and "We Are One in the Spirit." It was powerful because the Jesus Movement was in full swing, and Calvary was ground zero. There would be no other explanation than this. Music was essential for building a bridge that brought in the young people, but Pastor Chuck Smith's powerful biblical messages kept us there.

The bands loved performing at Calvary as an expression of their creativity and faith. That was all well and good, but creativity and faith didn't put food on the table. They needed to eat before they got there. They needed gas in the tank to drive them there. If they were going to continue, they needed to make an income off the music. So Chuck Smith created an avenue for this to work.

Enough acts passed through the church to form a record label, so that's exactly what Smith did. In 1971, he formed Maranatha! Music, a nonprofit Christian music record label to make what was heard in the church more widely available and provide an outlet for the talent that emerged from Calvary Chapel. The label's first official issue was called *The Everlastin' Living Jesus Music Concert* (1971). It wasn't a live concert album, but a sampler of various artists performing the best music coming out of Calvary Chapel. It sold more than two hundred thousand units, making a tidy return on the investment from the initial $4,000 it took to produce. It remains one of the most important releases in Contemporary Christian Music history. The songs and albums created through Maranatha! became the vanguard of Jesus Music and were the start of what we know as Contemporary Christian music.

In 1971, the media put its stamp on the countercultural embrace of the Son of God when *TIME* magazine published a cover story on "The Jesus Revolution," chronicling how young people were accepting Christ in big numbers. Other news outlets then began writing about the phenomenon.

Photos and news clips of Chuck Smith and Lonnie Frisbee baptizing hundreds of people in the Southern California surf spread across the print and broadcast worlds. But even though the hoopla would fade, the music would endure.

While there was a record label now publishing Jesus Music, it was a cottage industry that was fairytale small. Print runs were low—ten thousand units or less—and recording budgets weren't just shoestring, they were practically barefoot. One Maranatha! Music release was recorded for $900. Distribution was limited to church gift shops, Christian bookstores, mail orders, and even folding tables in Sunday School classrooms.

"We literally put those albums in a Sunday school room and priced them at $4.98, and people would buy them," said Love Song's Tommy Coomes. "(People) would buy five of them and give them to their friends."[2]

What this emerging music desperately needed was a launching pad. As it turned out, Dallas, Texas, would become Cape Canaveral for Contemporary Christian music with a festival and week-long conference: an event in June 1972 called Explo '72 (short for "Spiritual Explosion"). It was held in the Cotton Bowl and hosted by Bill Bright's Campus Crusade for Christ (now called Cru), and drew more than eighty thousand people from more than seventy-five countries to praise Jesus. It was referred to as the "religious Wood-stock" for Christian bands—with an assist from a handful of secular artists and a famed evangelist known to everyone simply as "Billy."

The lineup featured Larry Norman, Love Song, André Crouch & The Disciples, Randy Matthews, the Archers, Children of the Day, and Phil Keaggy. Also, there were "secular" stars including Johnny Cash, June Carter, Kris Kristofferson, and Rita Coolidge. Billy Graham—yes, *that* Billy—rocked the final night with a pow-erful keynote address.

"I wanted to come and identify with [the youth] because I believe this is a great and historic gathering," Graham told a televi-sion news reporter who asked why he was there. "This is going to be a moment in the history of Dallas and a moment in the history of the world."[3]

Having the famous (and infamous) Johnny Cash identify as "one of us" was a big deal. But Graham's presence was what added real legitimacy to the massive event and the new worship music being played there. Graham said Explo '72 was one of the greatest experiences of his life. It was a paradigmatic moment and one of the signature events of the Jesus Movement.

The timing was especially fortuitous for Love Song, whose self-titled debut album released the week before their big appearance. As a result, *Love Song* sold approximately two hundred thousand units, and the group later received an offer from Atlantic Records Cofounder and President, Ahmet Ertegun, to switch over to his label. The band refused because they were fine where they were, ministering to saved and unsaved souls alike through their music.

"For me, the key thing was Billy Graham got up and spoke," said Love Song's Chuck Girard. "Rock 'n roll is about rebellion and parents are like, 'Uh, this is so bad.' Billy gets up, speaks, and suddenly, he opened their minds to the idea that this music that's born out of rebellion . . . maybe this can be appropriated to something that the Holy Spirit can use. It was an indelible seal of approval."[4]

While audience members were mostly high school and college kids, a half-dozen record executives on hand saw the potential of a new and untapped market. Helping to bridge the gap were mainstream acts beginning to dip their toes into the Christian pool. B. J. Thomas, Barry McGuire, Glen Campbell, and Johnny Cash all had Christian hits on the singles charts.

Films like *Godspell*, *The Cross and the Switchblade*, Cash's film *The Gospel Road*, and *Jesus Christ Superstar* also rode the wave of Jesus mania. Some of these films, like *The Cross and the Switchblade*, were sincere but lacking the artistry needed to reach a larger audience. Others were entirely misleading, like *Jesus Christ Superstar*, which offered great music but got the story all wrong.

All of this didn't go unnoticed by the press, which gave it coverage in *Rolling Stone*, *LIFE*, *LOOK*, and a cover story in *TIME* magazine, one of America's most respected news publications at the time. As I said, they even gave it a name: "The Jesus Revolution." Its followers became known as "Jesus freaks."[5]

During those few years in the early 1970s, the name of Jesus seemed to be everywhere. We have not seen another Great Awakening since. But I do feel the time is ripe for one.

After the national media spotlight moved on, the Jesus freaks stuck around. They ditched the headbands and fringe jackets, and a lot of them even cut their hair. (Others lost theirs, me included.) Like a long-lasting marriage, while the initial ardor cooled, something more permanent took its place. It became rare for a church not to have a full band and a professional sound system. Music services were no longer three hymns and a benediction. Now, and likely forevermore, Contemporary Christian music is a mainstay for churches around the world.

The Jesus Movement that brought guitars, drums, and all types of modern instruments into sanctuaries is directly responsible for this. I believe it was a positive contribution for the church to reach the culture. And it's one of the best and most enduring parts of its legacy. In time, the movement would spread from the rock genre to include pop, rap, metal, gospel, country, alternative, and praise and worship.

Jesus was making an impact on the culture.

Larry Norman had it right when, in one of his lyrics, he asked, "Dear John: who's more popular now?"

CHAPTER FIVE

Another Face of Dylan

As I stated earlier in this book, if there were ever a Mount Rushmore of Rock, surely Bob Dylan would be one of the faces on it, along with Elvis Presley, John Lennon, and Paul McCartney.

Dylan is a musical chameleon known for hiding behind his Wayfarers and constantly changing his persona. He went from folk to electric rock, to being the prophet of protest, and from Nashville crooner to circus ringleader. But in 1979, he became a very unexpected and outspoken follower of Jesus Christ. He even issued three Gospel-infused albums to prove it. The first of the three, *Slow Train Coming*, I have always felt was some of his finest work artistically.

Throughout his career, fans and critics alike have struggled to figure out the enigmatic singer-songwriter. And even he agrees. Dylan once told a reporter, "My past has been so complicated, you wouldn't believe it, man."

Born as Robert Zimmerman in 1941 to Russian immigrants, he was raised in a solidly Jewish household in Hibbing, Minnesota.

His father, Abe, was the president of the local B'nai B'rith lodge. His mother, Beatrice, was the president of the local Hadassah chapter. Young Robert attended a Jewish camp each summer, studied Hebrew, and knew the pronunciations and meanings of four hundred Hebrew words.

"Literally, he could speak Hebrew like they do in Israel today," his father once said.[1]

He prepared for his bar mitzvah in 1954 and later joined a Jewish fraternity (Sigma Alpha Mu) while attending the University of Minnesota in Minneapolis. He visited Israel in 1969 and 1971, stopping at the Western Wall and a Kabbalistic training center in Jerusalem. Throughout the years, he donated money to Israel.

Nothing in his life ever indicated he would become a born-again Christian. Or did it?

Like everyone else in the 1960s countercultural movement, Dylan believed in subverting everything the previous generation had embraced as truth. But he did not spout mere clichés like "Make Love, Not War." Dylan's songs were intelligent, poetic, and powerful. People of all ages would pore over his lyrics, trying to figure out what he was really saying. There is no doubt that his songs often echoed biblical themes.

Soon, Dylan turned out to be a spokesperson for youth who wanted change and something different from the conformity of the previous decade, which many felt was repressive, stodgy, and dogmatic. He provided a soundtrack for all of that. Songs like "Blowin' in the Wind," "Like a Rolling Stone," and "Only a Pawn in Their Game" captured that desire for change.

He campaigned for civil rights (he sang at the March on Washington in 1963), women's rights, sexual liberation, rebellion against war, and generally anything anti-establishment. His music started out in the American folk tradition of Woody Guthrie but changed with the times. He didn't sing about striking miners or farms being washed away by floods, but about freedom, inequity, relationships, the loss of innocence, and fear of nuclear war. In 1965, he made the radical decision to appear at the Newport Folk Festival with an electric guitar (a Fender Stratocaster which recently sold for $1 million). The reaction was so negative that he left the stage after three songs; the folkies were upset because they could not let go of the acoustic-guitar-strumming, harmonica-playing Dylan.

That reaction was nothing compared to the reception he received when he released his first Christian album, *Slow Train Coming* (1979).

Dylan's conversion was not something that came on suddenly. It was more of a slow buildup over the years. In *Bob Dylan: A Spiritual Life*, author Scott Marshall notes that, of all Dylan's works from 1961 to 1978, eighty-nine of two hundred and forty-six songs or liner notes contain references to either the Hebrew scriptures or the New Testament, most notably "Knocking on Heaven's Door." Dylan readily admitted to reading the Bible but said up to that point, he "only looked at it as literature. I never read it in a way that was meaningful to me."

That changed later, in a big way.

Dylan's spiritual curiosity led him to seek the advice of rabbis and to watch a couple of live Billy Graham Crusades. Of the latter he said, "He was the greatest preacher and evangelist in my time—that guy could save souls and did. I went to two or three rallies in the 1950s and 1960s. He had the hair, the tone, and the elocution—when he spoke, he brought the storm down. Clouds parted. Souls got saved, sometimes thirty to forty thousand."[2]

During his legendary Rolling Thunder Tour between 1975 and 1976, Dylan attended a Christian outreach event at Peacock Park in Miami, Florida. He heard a hot Gospel message preached by

Arthur Blessitt, once known as "The Mod Minister of the Sunset Strip." Blessitt had a club in Hollywood called His Place, which was a psychedelic Gospel nightclub/coffeehouse situated next to a topless bar.

Dylan must have been touched, because he requested and was granted a private audience with Blessitt. It is reported that the two men made an instant connection that day. Blessitt later revealed that the rocker was curious about having a personal relationship with Jesus.

"(Dylan) asked how did I know Jesus was in my life; how did I know there was a God, and that He really cares; and how did I know Jesus was the right way? Our conversation was all about Jesus, not religion," recalled Blessitt, who later became famous for carrying a life-size cross through 324 nations, island groups, and territories around the globe. "He was wanting to know if Jesus was really the Way, the Truth, and the Life. I sought to answer the questions he asked as best as I could. The talk was very intense, and he was totally interested in Jesus."[3]

At the end of their chat, Blessitt prayed over Dylan, that he would come to know and follow Jesus.

Unlike most in the '60s counterculture, Dylan had not rejected faith completely. In November 1978, he had a legitimate spiritual metamorphosis after a fan tossed a necklace with a tiny silver cross onstage in San Diego to the legendary singer-songwriter. Dylan picked it up, placed it in his pocket, and forgot about it until the following night. Feeling a little melancholy and perhaps alone and isolated in his hotel room in Tucson, Arizona, he fished the necklace out of his pocket and placed it around his neck. It felt natural.

In reflection, Dylan said of that fateful night: "Now, I usually don't pick up things in front of the stage; occasionally I do, sometimes I don't. But I looked down at that cross. I said, 'I gotta pick up the cross and I put it in my pocket . . . I said, 'Well, I need something tonight.' I don't know what it was. I was used to all kinds of things. I said, 'I need something tonight that I didn't have before.' And I looked in my pocket and I had this cross . . ."[4]

The timing of this event coincided with the divorce and custody battle between Dylan and his first wife, Sara, and the recent conversions of his girlfriend, actress Mary Alice Artes, and bandmates Steven Soles and T-Bone Burnett. Artes was a Christian who had strayed from her faith and returned to it after attending a Vineyard Christian Fellowship meeting at the Beverly Hills Women's Club. The church was founded in 1974 by my friend Kenn Gulliksen, who was a part of the Jesus Movement at Calvary Chapel in Costa Mesa. Gulliksen felt called to reach people in the LA area, and The Vineyard was born.

Dylan even wrote a song about Artes, the reggae-influenced "Precious Angel." The song contains many biblical references, making a compelling case for Christ. Dylan writes of an angel who showed him—a blind man—to the light.

Artes and Dylan had been living with each other for some time by then, but her new commitment to Christ led her to move out; she wanted to lead a life that honored the Lord. The move blew Dylan away and nudged him a little closer toward the faith.

Through Artes's soft but firm prompting, Dylan eventually received Christ. He recalled it as "a knee-buckling experience" preceded by a long period of disillusionment.

He said: "Music wasn't like it used to be. We were filling halls, but I used to walk out on the street afterward and look up in the sky and know there is something else . . . a lot of people have died along the way—the Janises and the Jimis—people get cynical or comfortable in their own minds and that makes you die too, but God has chosen to revive me."[5]

Interesting that Dylan thought of two people he personally knew who, tragically, were part of the dreaded 27 Club.

In fact, Dylan said his rebirth was more than just spiritual—it was physical.

"Jesus put His hand on me," Dylan told journalist Karen Hughes. "It was a physical thing. I felt it. I felt it all over me. I felt my whole body tremble. The glory of the Lord knocked me down and picked me up."[6]

He spent five months in intense Bible study with eleven other students under the discipleship of several Vineyard pastors. One of the students was Jennifer Yaffee (Goetz), whom I have known for decades.

Jennifer was twenty-two years old when she toured with Dylan on the Rolling Thunder Revue, which traversed the United States and Canada between 1975 and 1976. In 1978, she went on another six-week Dylan tour of Europe.

"Traveling with Bob, I met some of the most famous people in the movie and music industry, got to hang out with people like Joni Mitchell and Joan Baez. I also witnessed some interesting things on that tour, including psychics, a palm reader, a tarot card reader, a tight-rope walker. It was like a crazy carnival," said Jennifer, who today works full-time with her husband, Marty Goetz, a talented and well-known Jewish gospel singer. "I noticed that Bob was fascinated by everything. He was curious about things and entertained lots of thoughts."

They stayed in luxury hotels, visited movie sets, and traveled in private caravans. Despite the wonder of it all, Jennifer was thoroughly depressed by the time it was over. She said she felt empty and believes Dylan must have felt the same way.

"Bob and I ended up getting saved in late 1978, and we both attended discipleship school together," Jennifer said. "We went four hours a day, five days a week for five months. It was intense, but we both really wanted to be there."[7]

Jennifer often cleaned the Brentwood, California, house Dylan shared at the time with his childhood friend Louie Kemp. "While Bob was getting deeper into the Bible, Louie was getting deeper into Judaism," she recalled. "I know that was a pull for Bob and there was a tug-of-war going on between the two of them."

Even though he was skeptical at first, Dylan was taught at The Vineyard to read the Bible in a way that was meaningful. He learned that both the Old and New Testaments have been given to us from God and speak to us in our daily lives.

Slow Train Coming was released after he completed that course.

"There's no question . . . in my mind that Bob had an absolute bona fide, real conversion," said Dave Kelly, a personal assistant of Dylan's who witnessed all this firsthand. "He had an epiphany. He had an experience where he recognized that Jesus was the Messiah, the Jewish Messiah. No question in my mind that it was real. It was not fake, and it was not a game."[8]

Jennifer also agreed it was a real conversion.

"He was very devoted to the class, and he came every day. He would ask questions from the Old Testament, and he participated," she said. "He would not have devoted all that time to the class if he weren't serious. I do believe he was born again, and that Jesus worked His way into his heart."

That said, Jennifer believed Dylan had a few behaviors that went unchecked.

"Bob once said to me, 'God knows that I've lived a very different life and I don't think He expects me to live like other people do,'" she recalled. But "there is no hierarchy in the Kingdom, and I don't think he was held accountable. I don't know if Bob ever recognized that, but I did."[9]

None of this happened in the public eye. Dylan's legions of fans still looked at him as the voice of protest. Their establishment. And he was.

After the rock revolution, "status quo" for many became "sex, drugs, and rock and roll." Obviously, that message was not necessarily one of morality, family, and faith in God. In due time, these baby boomers would become the adults who would run our country and influence the culture.

So, for Bob Dylan, spokesman for a generation, to become a believer in Jesus Christ and someone who believed the Bible was, in fact, the most countercultural act of his entire career up to that point. He was the ultimate rebel, and not just because he played electric guitar and wore shades. He was rebelling against a culture that in some ways he had helped to create.

That would be reflected in the most controversial album of his career.

Slow Train Coming went platinum, outselling both his classic albums *Blood on the Tracks* and *Blonde on Blonde*. Critics gave it mixed reviews, but most were negative. *Rolling Stone* editor Jan Wenner was an exception, calling it, "one of the finest records Dylan has ever made," but others called the album bitter and angry.

Greil Marcus of *The Village Voice* said, "The album chilled the soul." A third critic, Charles Shaar Murray of Britain's *New Musical Express*, summed up the contradiction when he wrote, "Bob Dylan has never seemed more perfect and more impressive than on this album. He has also never seemed more unpleasant and hate-filled." This statement reveals the bias of the reviewer. Nothing could have been further from the truth. Dylan was simply continuing to provide that prophetic voice to his generation, but now it was based on a more reliable source than his mere opinion; it was based on what the Bible says. However, many of Dylan's fans were not buying it. That said, Dylan gained legions of new fans who were listening to him for the first time.

In his newfound exuberance, Dylan refused to play his older songs, or indeed any secular material at all. The church, through Larry Myers, pastor of a Vineyard congregation in Los Angeles, told Dylan his old songs were okay—they weren't sacrilegious. But Dylan refused to budge, saying he would not "sing any song which hasn't been given to me by the Lord to sing."

Fans relentlessly heckled him at concerts, even carrying signs declaring "Jesus Loves Your Old Music." Others chanted, "We want Bob Dylan! Where's Bob Dylan?" They were answered by mini-sermons from the stage, with Dylan telling his fans they were now living in the end times and Jesus was coming back. Whatever high they had coming into the venue was gone by the end of the show. Bob Dylan had something to say. Moreover, he had a platform from which to say it, and he was going to use it.

After a two-week residency at the Fox Warfield Theatre in San Francisco, California, a newspaper headline blared: "Bob Dylan: His Born-Again Show's a Real Drag."

Consider the times and context of Dylan's conversion. The heyday of the hippies was long gone. Disco was ascending. There was no truth in drugs; everyone knew that now. But it really didn't matter. Everyone still wanted to get high. People were tired of being miserable. They were miserable about domestic terrorism. Miserable about Watergate. Inflation had given everyone a beating. A recession was in full swing. American hostages were being held in Iran, the Russians were breathing down our necks, and the whole country was exhausted. Even President Jimmy Carter noted in his "Crisis of Confidence Speech" in July 1979, that "we can see this crisis in the growing doubt of the meaning of our own lives and in the loss of unity and purpose as a nation. The erosion of confidence in the future is threatening to destroy the social and political fabric of the nation."[10]

"Malaise" is the word that sums up that time in American history.

The stage was set for the curtain to reopen on a new morning in America, which Ronald Reagan would later bring. Tie dyes were being replaced by neckties. Hair was cut and slicked back. And it was time to make some money, honey. Lennon's line "Imagine no possessions" was replaced by "Greed is good!" as expressed by Michael Douglas's character, Gordon Gekko, in the Oliver Stone film *Wall Street*. The drug of the zeitgeist was cocaine, which matched the country's mood perfectly. Get high, work hard, party all night, and do it again the next day.

Therefore, no one wanted to listen to Dylan deliver a lecture from the Bible, but Bob was on point with exactly the message America needed to hear.

My wife Cathe and I personally witnessed this at a show at the Santa Monica Civic Center in November 1979. When *Slow Train Coming* was released, the new Dylan stood up for all the world to see: I could hardly believe that he had become a Christian. I knew about the many biblical references and allusions in his songs, but this was a shock to the system. Dylan was the ultimate anti-establishment voice, a "don't follow leaders" kind of guy. But now he was following the ultimate Leader, even hosting backstage prayer meetings before each show. To have Dylan profess his faith in Christ was the rock equivalent of the conversion of Saul of Tarsus two thousand years earlier.

And like Saul in Damascus, Dylan was treated like a traitor in Santa Monica that night. The auditorium was nowhere near sold out, and the people who did show up were booing and heckling him to no end.

"Sing 'Blowin' in the Wind'!" they'd shout. Or "Do 'Like a Rolling Stone.'"

I winced when they did that, but respected Dylan for sticking to his guns and singing only his Christian material. The only respite from the hatred he received during that period was when his song "Gotta Serve Somebody" from *Slow Train Coming* won a Grammy for Best Rock Vocal Performance by a Male and a Dove Award for, ironically, Best Album by a Secular Artist. But those were the only accolades.

The criticism didn't stop with the press. John Lennon, who had great admiration for Dylan, as reflected in his songs "You've Got to Hide Your Love Away" and "In My Life," joined in the chorus of mockery by penning a profanity-laced parody of Dylan's "Serve Somebody," called "Serve Yourself." Among the other things, John sang about believing in devils, lords, and Christ. In a diary tape from September 5, 1979, Lennon was recorded as saying: "'Gotta Serve Somebody' . . . guess [Dylan] wants to be a waiter now."

Keith Richards, the legendary Rolling Stones guitarist, was even more cutting. He cynically stated to a reporter that he thought Dylan's conversion was simply made to change things up artistically and perhaps even make a buck. He called Dylan "the prophet of profit." (Keep in mind, these two were friends!)

But an April 1980 letter to a fan named "Steve" showed that Dylan was serious.

"We are up in Toronto singing and playing for about three thousand people a night in a downtown theatre," Dylan wrote. "The Spirit of the Lord is calling people here in their beautiful and clean city, but they are more interested in lining up for *Apocalypse Now* than to be baptized and filled with the Holy Ghost."[11]

By that point Dylan's record label, Columbia, was fed up. Deputy President Dick Asher read the superstar the riot act. He screamed at

Dylan, "No Torah! No Bible! No Quran! No Jesus! No God! No Allah! No religion. It's going to be in the contract!"[12]

It didn't appear that Dylan listened to Asher's ultimatum. During his next tour he often quoted Scripture. He informed an audience in Albuquerque, New Mexico, one night: "I told you, 'the times they are a-changin', and they did. I said the answer was 'blowin' in the wind,' and it was. I'm telling you now that Jesus is coming back, and He is! And there is no other way of salvation . . . Jesus is coming back to set up His Kingdom in Jerusalem for a thousand years."[13]

Dylan was telling the truth, and a lot of people did not like it. But over his next two albums, he doubled down. *Saved* (1980) and *Shot of Love* (1981) expanded on the biblical themes of his conversion.

Saved was soundly bashed by the rock media again, including *Rolling Stone*, which declared, "Dylan's clunky fervor . . . only made him sound ridiculous." Critic Kurt Loder wrote, "Dylan hadn't simply found Jesus, but seemed to imply that he had his home phone number as well."

But Dylan had indeed found something better than the empty life of rock stardom: a personal relationship with God through Jesus Christ. This is what the young Bobby Zimmerman had been searching for in his youth. This is what his earlier classic songs were pointing toward. Now that he had found it, most people did not want to hear about it. In fact, they resented him—even hated him—for expressing it.

Shot of Love carried that theme of persecution, an answer to the heckling and abuse that Dylan took at concerts now. The rhetorical stoning of Bob Dylan seemed to be everyone's favorite pastime. People went to his concerts specifically to deliver verbal brickbats and stick it to the man who was now The Man. The song "Property of Jesus" is the tortured cry of a person mocked for his faith. (In the end, he doesn't mind because he's "the property of Jesus.")

Fans were not the only angry demographic. Some Jewish people felt that Dylan had abandoned his roots. They were disgusted by his Gospel preaching and rejected his Christian messages. Others said he never lost his roots during this period. Seth Rogovoy, author of *Bob Dylan: Prophet, Mystic, Poet*, said *Slow Train Coming* did not show a full commitment to Christianity. "There is stuff that is very Jewish on the album and stuff that comes directly from Jewish scripture." Rogovoy saw *Slow Train Coming* as Dylan exploring R&B and gospel and making them his own.

There was more than an ounce of truth to what Rogovoy wrote, as Dylan seemed to return to Orthodox Judaism in 1982. By then he had cut ties with Artes. He had great hopes for their relationship, but she had moved to the East Coast to resume her acting career. He bought her a $25,000 engagement ring, but she did not want to marry him.

As usual, Dylan's beliefs came out in his songs. One particular track, "Neighborhood Bully," from 1983's *Infidels*, has been called rock's most Zionist song. His Christian phase was not as pronounced, but he never denied it.

"Jesus Himself only preached for three years," Dylan told the *Los Angeles Times*[14]—roughly the same amount of time Dylan was more outspoken about his newfound faith.

A year later, he greatly expanded on his core spirituality in a lengthy interview with *Rolling Stone's* Kurt Loder. He said he literally believed the Bible. He felt the Old and New Testaments were equally valid and claimed the only church or synagogue he belonged to was "the church of the poisoned mind," no doubt a tongue-in-cheek reference to the hit from Culture Club by the same name.

He said he could converse and find agreement with both Christians and Orthodox Jews.

Fact is, I could say the same thing. I have friends who are Orthodox Jews with whom I have much in common. Dylan said the failure of his trilogy of Christian albums to appeal to audiences was not because of the material.

"The people who reacted to the gospel stuff would've reacted that way if I hadn't done, you know, 'Song to Woody,'" he said.[15]

Dylan wrote in the 2020 song "I Contain Multitudes" that he was a man of contradictions and many moods. I'll say.

As I wrote earlier, the Bible says, "We live our lives like a story being told." These chapters from Dylan's life are significant.

Four decades and many chapters later, Dylan's story is still unfolding. He still charts new territory. Over the last twenty years, he's released rockabilly, swing, jazz, blues, and lounge music albums. He even snagged a 2016 Nobel Prize in literature. Well-deserved, I would say. He continues to tour approximately one hundred nights a year.

When Dylan released *Christmas in the Heart* (2009), an interviewer named Bill Flanagan took notice of his authentic delivery on "O Little Town of Bethlehem."

"I don't want to put you on the spot, but you sure deliver that song like a true believer," Flanagan said.

"Well, I am a true believer," Dylan replied nonchalantly.[16]

The furor over Dylan's spirituality is mostly in the past. Every few years there's a new interview, and the questions about his faith arise. He usually gives a noncommittal answer, saying in the end it's all about the music.

"I find the religiosity and philosophy in the music. . . . The songs are my lexicon," Dylan once said. "I believe in the songs."[17]

It seems that everyone except Dylan has had a problem with this ambiguity, mostly his critics.

Perhaps a conversation with Dylan's former wife, Carolyn Dennis, will bring some clarity about whether the enigmatic entertainer is Jewish or Christian. She said, "I noticed a Bible in his room one day as he was packing. Amidst all the rumors that he was no longer a Christian, I asked him if he was still a believer. His answer was short and simple: 'I believe the whole Bible.'"[18]

The simple answer to the riddle of Robert Zimmerman may simply be this: He is Jewish. He is a Christian. He was born Jewish, and he was "born again" to be a Christian. Being a Christian does not mean you no longer are Jewish. Jesus was Jewish. The Apostles were as well, including the Apostle Paul. It was to a well-known, deeply religious man and Jewish leader named Nicodemus that Jesus said, "You must be born again." Bob Dylan certainly seemed to have that experience and has never denied it. So why should we question it?

Like you and me, Bob Dylan is a work in progress. I pray that he grows in his faith and perhaps publicly talks about it more in the days ahead. On his latest record, *Rough and Rowdy Ways* (2020), Dylan hardly hides his Gospel leanings. His song "I've Made Up My Mind to Give Myself to You" makes that clear. On another track, "Goodbye, Jimmy Reed," Dylan sings about the Kingdom, the power, and the glory of God.

Yes, it appears that, to Bob Dylan, the Gospel is still "the real story." Though many of Bob's generation are gone now—many of whom he directly influenced—Dylan is still here.

And he is still a prophetic voice to this generation.

CHAPTER SIX

Help Me If You Can, I'm Feeling Down

At the start of the 1970s, the Beatles broke up and John Lennon famously wrote that "God is a concept by which we measure our own pain." He also wrote that he didn't believe in Elvis, Zimmerman (Bob Dylan), Buddha, Kennedy, the Beatles, or the Bible. At that period of his life, the ex-Beatle didn't believe in anything, but he sampled everything.

He became a spiritual tourist, dropping in on many different traditions, though never committing to any one of them.

"I believe in everything until it's disproved," Lennon once said. "So I believe in fairies, the myths, dragons. It all exists, even if it's in your mind. Who's to say that dreams and nightmares aren't as real as the here and now?"[1]

He had already explored Transcendental Meditation with the rest of the Beatles in India, and over time he sponsored International Society for Krishna Consciousness founder A. C. Bhaktivedanta Swami Prabhupada and a smorgasbord of other Hare Krishna devotees at his eighty-acre English country estate.

For a while, he emoted with the Primal Scream crowd—a form of psychotherapy in which the patient recalls and reenacts disturbing experiences and then rears back and lets it rip.

At the same time, Lennon embraced radical ideas from the counterculture, which were so widespread that they really weren't radical at all—such as the anti-war and Women's Liberation movements, as well as Native and African American rights, conservation, and prison reform. However, his behavior landed him on Richard Nixon's Enemies List and in J. Edgar Hoover's FBI files. But there was nothing suspicious about it. He either was associated with or openly funded people like Black Power leader Michael X (convicted of murder, he was executed by hanging in 1975), Black Panther cofounder Bobby Seale, beat poet Allen Ginsberg, and Chicago Seven defendants Abbie Hoffman and Jerry Rubin. He also spent time with a Greenwich Village busker named David Peel, producing his 1972 album *The Pope Smokes Dope*. If you were a hippie rock star celebrity at that time, these were certainly the people you'd hang out with.

As crazy as this sounds, some people believe Lennon may have written a letter to the legendary charismatic television preacher Oral Roberts. No one would ever describe Roberts as "radical," but a copy of this letter allegedly is kept at the Tulsa-based university bearing his name. (My co-author Marshall Terrill asked for a photocopy of the letter during the writing of this book to verify the rumor one way or the other; the university refused to provide one.)

Students at Oral Roberts University pledged not to drink, smoke, or have premarital sex. Lennon did all three and then some. One would think that Roberts would be the last person Lennon would approach for advice.

At the time, Lennon was at the tail end of his political-activist phase, supporting progressive and radical causes. He lent his name and invested his money to many left-wing causes, participating in street demonstrations and shouting slogans through a megaphone. He used his craft and fame to push social and political change.

"John was a pacifist and once told me that he would run off to Ireland if he was to report for National Service in the British Army," said Ivor Davis, a journalist for London's *Daily Express* who toured with the Beatles in 1964 and knew Lennon both personally and professionally. "He also made *How I Won the War*, an anti-war and counterculture film."[2]

The bespectacled Beatle even wrote the ultimate anti-war song in "Give Peace a Chance," which half a million people sang outside the gates of the White House shortly after President Richard Nixon took office. It didn't go unnoticed by those in charge.

But Lennon's world came crashing down on November 7, 1972. That's when Richard Nixon handily defeated George McGovern in his reelection bid for president. That was the first election in which eighteen-year-olds were given the right to vote, and Nixon feared that they were likely to be anti-war and pro-McGovern. Lennon's new friend, professional rabble-rouser Jerry Rubin, felt that Lennon could unify these youth if he agreed to headline a national concert tour that would coincide with the election season, combining rock with voter registration. Nixon feared Lennon's influence and moved to deport the ex-Beatle on a past marijuana bust in England. Ultimately, the tour never took place because Lennon so frequently found himself in immigration court.

"The last thing on earth I want to do is perform," Lennon later said. "That's a direct result of the immigration thing. In '71, '72, I wanted to go out and rock onstage and I just stopped."[3]

Nixon's landslide victory devastated Lennon. He felt it struck a major blow to his chances of staying in the country. He got loaded on tequila that night in a blowout at Jerry Rubin's funky East Village apartment on Prince Street in New York City. It took a dark turn when Lennon, who was swigging from a bottle at that point, began screaming and cursing.

"I don't want to be John and Yoko anymore. I'm through, I had enough, I can't stand it, I don't want her," Lennon said. Then he looked directly at his wife, Yoko Ono, and said, "I don't want you." This fight led to a very public separation that lasted almost eighteen months.

The letter Lennon supposedly penned to Roberts in November 1972 had more than an air of desperation. It read:

Rev. Roberts:
This is ex-Beatle John Lennon. I have been waiting to write to you, but I guess I didn't really want to face reality. I never do so this is why I take drugs; reality frightens me and paranoids me. True I have a lot of money, being a Beatle, been all around the world but basically, I am afraid to face the problems of life. Let me begin to say I regret it that I said "The Beatles" were more popular than Jesus. I don't even like myself anymore. Guilt.

My cousin Marilyn McCabe has tried to help me she told me you were praying for me.

Here's my life. Born in Liverpool. My mum died when I was little. My father left me at three. It was rough cause just my aunt raised me. I never really liked her. I had an unhappy childhood, depressed a lot. Always missing my mom. Maybe if I had a father like you, I would have been a better person. My own father, I hate with a passion because he left my and mom and me. He came to me after we filmed A Hard Day's Night and asked for some money. It made me so mad Paul M. had to hold me down I was going to kill him. I was under the influence of Pills at the time.

I was brought up a Catholic. Never went along with their teachings.

Married Cynthia had a son Julian. I had to marry her. I really never loved her. She always embarrassed me, walking around pregnant, not married; so, I married her. Only one regret Julian has had to suffer a lot cause recently she's been married again. He and me never get to see each other. Cause she refuses cause I'm married to Yoko.

So, life as a Beatle hasn't been all that great. I came out and told them I wanted a divorce cause Paul and me never got along anymore. And that's how the four ended.

Since 1967 I have had a police record for dope and forging traveler's checks to America.

My wife Yoko and I have searched all over for her daughter we can't find. Her ex-husband took her away. Yoko's going crazy.

As the song we wrote is that we wrote, Paul and me, "Money Can't Buy Me Love," it's true.

The point is this I want happiness; I don't want to keep up with drugs. Paul told me once you make fun of me for not taking drugs, but you'll regret it in the end.

Explain to me, what Christianity can do for me. Is it phony, can He love me? I want out of Hell!

P.S. This address, staying at the cousin's house.

Rev Roberts Also,

I did watch your show until Channel 6 took it off of the air. Please try to get it back on. A lot of older people I know loved your show.

I especially liked the World Action Singers; your son Richard is a real good singer. George told me he met you and them when he was at the studio.

Sincerely,

John

P.S. I am I hate to say it under the influence of pills now. I can't stop. I only wish I could thank you for caring.[4]

Many Beatles historians decry the authenticity of this letter, but during his lifetime, Lennon never openly disputed its contents or the fact that Oral Roberts publicly mentioned it in one of his sermons shortly after it came into his possession. Perhaps Lennon didn't want to give the story any legs. I'm not entirely convinced the letter is the real deal, but it's interesting to contemplate.

It certainly fits Lennon's mindset at the time—dabbling in anything spiritual, no matter how far out or offbeat. That includes turning to psychics, witchcraft, and the occult, which he started to do with more frequency in the mid-1970s. Yoko had hired a psychic named John Green for $25,000 a year, whom Lennon called "Charlie Swan." Living rent-free in one of the Lennons' investment properties—a Soho loft—Green was on call twenty-four hours a day. He read the couple's tarot cards, dispensing advice on anything from investments and travel to new hires, old friends, and whatever other problems they felt were pressing at the time.

Lennon shouldn't have felt pressed by anything. He withdrew from the music business in 1975, the year his contract with Apple Records came to an end. Most of his legal entanglements had been settled—including his immigration case, which had dragged on for almost five years. On October 7, 1975, the U.S. Court of Appeals in New York overturned the order from the Immigration and

Naturalization Service to deport Lennon and granted him permanent residency to live in the United States. He told reporters of the decision, "I feel higher than the Empire State Building."[5] Two days later, on October 9—Lennon's thirty-fifth birthday—son Sean Taro Ono Lennon was born.

At that point in his life, the former Beatle formally entered his "househusband" stage, staying out of the public eye for the latter half of the decade. Fully ensconced inside the Dakota, the iconic New York City apartment building where the Lennons resided on the seventh floor in Apartment 72, he baked bread, changed diapers, and fed and bathed Sean during the day while Yoko ran their business affairs from an office below. With plenty of nannies to care for Sean, Lennon was free to putter around the house and indulge his every whim. Mostly, he spent his time in his bedroom, avoiding the legion of staff members that included assistants, psychics, astrologists, masseuses, maids, acupuncturists, and handymen. When he closed the door behind him, he mostly read, drew cartoons, wrote lyrics or little stories, watched TV, or got stoned on pot or magic mushrooms. His ambition waned and he was simply passing the time. He sang about this phase in his classic song, "Watching the Wheels."

On January 1, 1975, Lennon began keeping a diary, and he continued to journal until December 8, 1980—the day he died. Robert Rosen, author of *Nowhere Man: The Final Days of John Lennon*, is one of only a handful of people who saw Lennon's private, handwritten diaries. He not only transcribed them but committed much of them to memory.

"(Lennon) would write virtually every single day in his *New Yorker* desk diaries and was very committed to this," Rosen said. "He really got into it, and parts of them were very stream of consciousness. In 1977 and 1978, he spent a lot of time sleeping and programming dreams. He got into a thing where he detailed every single dream."[6]

When Lennon wasn't sleeping or blissed out, he explored yoga, fasting, mysticism, vegetarianism, and various forms of religion. (Near the end of his life, he referred to himself as a "Zen pagan.")

But then the unexpected happened. Some would say the impossible took place.

The man who once said the Beatles were more popular than Jesus apparently came to Jesus Himself in the spring of 1977 after watching a televised Billy Graham Crusade. Rosen recalled, "[Lennon] was watching Billy Graham sermons on TV because he found them entertaining. Then he had an epiphany. Apparently, Graham's words got through to him and he accepted Jesus. It drove him to tears of joy and ecstasy. He was born again.

"It lasted about two weeks."[7]

In that two-week period, the former Beatle considered himself a Christian and took his wife and their child to an Easter Sunday service. He even called the prayer line of *The 700 Club*, Pat Robertson's evangelistic network. This new spark in Lennon's life inspired him to write a song called "Amen," which was his musical version of "The Lord's Prayer."

"I remember Lennon drew a crucifix in his diary during this period and was always writing, 'Thank you, Jesus' or 'Thank you, Lord,'" Rosen recalled. "He tried to get Yoko Ono into it, and she wasn't interested. He later apologized for subjecting her to Billy Graham, so it just came and went."[8]

But there's some evidence that Lennon's Christian phase might have lasted a little longer than those two weeks. In May 1977, the Lennons, with two-year-old son Sean and a pair of assistants in tow, headed to the Far East to visit Yoko's parents, whom they hadn't seen in almost six years. They spent a few weeks in Hong

Kong and Tokyo before heading ninety-five miles northwest to the alpine resort town of Karuizawa, the Onos' ancestral home. They stayed at the Mampei Hotel, a luxury resort and mountain lodge off the evergreen slopes of Mount Asama.

The Lennons spent most mornings taking leisurely bike rides with Sean (his child's seat was attached to John's handlebars) through the Japanese mountains, boat rides on a nearby lake, visits to Shiraito Waterfall, or having picnics and tossing a frisbee around. One day, as they rode bikes, John and Yoko came across signs laced with yellow ribbons on the town's main street, which was filled with eateries, galleries, and shops that sold cherry wood carvings and kokeshi dolls.

"Follow this line to Heaven," declared one sign. "Come to the Power and Light," read another inviting people for free coffee, cake, and conversation in English.[9]

Intrigued, the Lennons followed the signs to a coffeehouse run by Christian missionaries Steven and Carol Fleenor. The two had moved to Karuizawa in 1971 to work at the summer camp Steven's parents had established in the 1950s. The camp worked with the Union Church, an interdenominational missionary church where they often held outdoor evangelistic meetings, reaching many Japanese people with the message of Christ.

Carol Fleenor recalled a long-haired, unshaven man with wire-rimmed glasses and sporting a wide-brimmed hat pedaling toward her.

"How you doing?" he shouted, waving at her. She thought he was a run-of-the mill hippie and dismissed him as she walked up the street with her family in tow. Lennon coasted past, she recalled, vanishing down the road. He seemed somewhat familiar to her, but she couldn't quite place the face. About a minute later, another bicycle coasted past: a Japanese woman with long, dark hair. Carol knew in an instant it was Yoko Ono. There was no mistaking that face. The hippie, she deduced, was John Lennon. What she didn't have the answer to was what they were doing in Karuizawa.[10]

The Lennons must have heard about the service at Union Church the following Sunday. It was packed. Midway through the sermon, Carol heard murmuring behind her. She strained her neck to see a man and a woman walking down the aisle, looking for a pair of open seats. The ruckus made the minister clear his throat and everyone snapped to attention. Carol could no longer focus for wonder of what the Lennons were doing there.

She would find out a few days later when two people on bicycles pedaled into her yard. "I saw your signs on the *machi* (the main street) and thought they were clever," Lennon said, breaking the ice. "I was telling [Yoko] that we needed to see what it was all about."[11]

Camp volunteers spotted the couple and suddenly gathered around to listen in on the conversation. John informed them he was on vacation and visiting Yoko's parents. The pleasantries nearly came to an end when one woman pushed to the front and was blunt to the point of rudeness.

"I read about your divorce. How could you leave your first marriage?" she asked. "What are you doing now that the Beatles have broken up?"[12]

Lennon remained calm and politely smiled. He gently told the woman that he was putting his music career on hold to spend time with his family. Carol Fleenor recalled the rude woman wasn't satisfied with the answer and probed a little more. Did Lennon belong to a church?

"Of course," he replied, laughing. "I'm C of E." The puzzled look on her face prompted Lennon to explain, "The Church of England. Haven't you heard of them?"[13]

More questions were fired at the ex-Beatle, who stood his ground and answered every one in a kind and polite manner—even when someone demanded to know how he could say the Beatles were more popular than Jesus Christ.

"When we talk to reporters, we play around with them," he explained. "We're just a music group. Don't people know that Jesus is far greater than we are?" That answer seemed to quell the small group.

Before he pedaled off, Lennon bid a fond farewell. "It's good to talk to all of you," he said. "I've been looking for something this summer, something spiritual. I've been speaking with a lot of the missionaries I've met here about life and what it all means. Thank you for your words."[14]

Years later, Carol Fleenor reflected on that fateful meeting with the Lennons.

"I had made all sorts of assumptions about John Lennon—that he was arrogant, disrespectful, antireligious, a rebellious hippie," she said. "But the man I met was none of those things. In fact, he was modest and self-effacing. Not like my idea of a rock star at all!

"I never did speak to John again. But I hope we helped him that summer. He certainly helped me. He reminded me of why I had come to Japan in the first place—to welcome people, not to judge them. And to grow in my understanding of the world."[15]

When the Lennons returned to New York, they left behind the brief peace they had known in Asia. John was depressed and melancholy from not making music. A series of unfortunate events would soon leave him bouncing around like the shiny chrome sphere in a pinball machine.

A terrorist threatened the family with bombing. The FALN—a clandestine organization dedicated to the political independence of Puerto Rico—demanded $100,000 from him and threatened to kill his family. The Lennons contacted the FBI, who spent a few months trying to track down the extortionists. To this day, the FBI cannot say whether the person has ever been identified or arrested.

The episode made the former Beatle paranoid and afraid to go out in public. Bucolic upstate New York seemed to offer a pleasant change from the *sturm und drang* of the city. The Lennons bought a thousand acres of farmland, intending to raise cattle. They also purchased a fourteen-thousand-square-foot, Mediterranean-style estate in Palm Beach, Florida, to mellow out in the summers.

That went off the rails when Lennon's first wife, Cynthia, published her memoir. *A Twist of Lennon* claimed he was an absentee father to their son Julian and had spent the last few years of their marriage lit on LSD. It wasn't a fabrication, but Lennon didn't want the information coming to light. He fought the book's publication in London's High Court but lost.

Lennon's tarot card reader then heard about a clandestine dig in Egypt to unearth an ancient temple. The rock star's trip to loot ancient treasures and an attempt to write a Broadway play were never fully formed, and eventually went sideways.

In May 1979, the Lennons took out a full-page ad in papers in London, New York, Los Angeles, and Tokyo titled "A Love Letter from John and Yoko to People Who Ask Us What, When, and Why." It basically explained why he hadn't produced any music in four years. This gave rise to rumors of a comeback or a possible Beatles reunion, which Lennon then had to respond to.

"He was a complicated person who was full of contradictions," Rosen recalled. "Part of him longed to follow The Way—the path of Jesus, Ghandi, Mohammad, and Buddha. The other half longed for the carnal pleasures of life like food, sex, and drugs. He was torn between those two things. He was also going, it seemed, in two directions."[16]

But there was something looming that no one, least of all Lennon himself, could see coming.

It started with the Lennons buying another house in Cold Spring Harbor on Long Island's Gold Coast, where John learned to sail. In May 1980, the tarot card reader told them that Lennon should journey in a southeasterly direction. (Bermuda lies southeast of New York.) Lennon promptly chartered a forty-three-foot sloop based in Newport, Rhode Island, for a five-day trip. The crew consisted of the captain and owner Hank Halstead (a former rock promoter), Lennon's sailing teacher from Cold Spring Harbor, and his teacher's two cousins. Lennon, being the least experienced in sailing, volunteered to be the cook.

Forty-eight hours into the journey, a brutal Force 8 gale hit. The teacher and his two cousins were taken down by severe sea sickness. Halstead manned the helm for forty-eight consecutive hours, giving Lennon the feel for keeping the ship safe in heavy seas as huge waves broke over the deck. Then, exhausted, there was nothing Halstead could do but hand the wheel over to Lennon.

"Jeez, Hank," Lennon told him, "all I've got are these skinny little guitar-playing muscles."[17] Halstead told Lennon to focus on the horizon, not the compass, then went below to pass out in his wet berth.

Like a character out of a Joseph Conrad or Samuel Taylor Coleridge novel, Lennon lashed himself to the wheel so he wouldn't be washed away by the relentless white waves pounding over the boat. The ship staggered up the faces of twenty-foot swells and surfed down the backs of them. He was completely alone. It was him against nature at its angriest.

"I was buried underwater," he recalled later.

I was smashed in the face for six hours. It's an incredible experience because it won't go away, you know, you can't change your mind . . . a couple of the waves had me on my knees; I was just hanging on with me hands on the wheel, but I did have rope around me to the side, but it was very powerful weather. And I had the time of my life—I was screamin' sea shanties and shoutin' at the gods, I felt like a Viking, you know, Jason and the Golden Fleece.[18]

It may have been the most cathartic and significant six hours of Lennon's life. When Halstead came back on deck, he was shocked by what he found.

"I met a different guy," Halstead said. "He was totally washed, exuberant, ecstatic." It was remarkable that a novice sailor kept the ship safe for so long under those conditions. "What an accomplishment," Halstead said later.[19]

It appeared that a new John Lennon was born from the sea and salt spray. He later described the voyage as "the most fantastic experience I ever had."

Upon docking in Bermuda, Lennon immediately decided to stay, rent a house, and write music. His muse had returned.

"Once I got there, I was so centered after the experience at sea that I was tuned in or whatever, to the cosmos," Lennon recalled. "And all these songs came."[20]

The result was 1980's *Double Fantasy*, his most accessible work in years. To be totally frank, I was not a fan of most of Lennon's solo work up to that point. When he and Paul McCartney matched up, they were without equals. Together they had written approximately two hundred songs, many of them iconic. Lennon would write something like "Strawberry

Fields Forever," and McCartney would answer with a song like "Penny Lane." One was cynical and mystical; the other buoyant and upbeat. They fed off each other and had alchemy that was off the charts. Much of that was lost when they headed their separate ways.

Lennon's post-Beatles material was hit and miss, and most of it had a painful feel to it—especially *Plastic Ono Band* (1970). I understood his pain. As stated in the letter to Oral Roberts, Lennon's mother, Julia, was killed by a drunk driver when he was a teen and he was raised by his Aunt Mimi, a rigid disciplinarian. His father, Freddie, was not a part of his life until Lennon had reached global success; John kept him at a distance. I can connect with this part of his story because I never knew my father, and my mom was a carefree and disconnected woman like Julia.

Conversely, I loved *Double Fantasy* because songs like "Starting Over" and "Woman" recaptured some of the Beatles' magic of days gone by. There was also a sweetness to "Beautiful Boy," which John wrote for Sean. Surprisingly, the man who a decade earlier had sung that he no longer believed in God now sang, "Before you go to sleep, say a little prayer."

Julian, John's son from his first marriage, admitted to feeling jealous over the attention his father showered on Sean, resulting in some tension throughout the years between the two half-brothers. But Yoko Ono did ask Julian to come to New York City in the immediate aftermath of John's death. Happily, both Sean and Julian have drawn closer as they've grown older and were together in November 2021 at the premiere of *The Beatles: Get Back*, a three-part documentary series brilliantly edited by director Peter Jackson.

Back to John Lennon: Did his beliefs change later in his life?

I believe he had matured. But according to one of the last major interviews he gave, Lennon said he was no more a Buddhist than he was a Christian.

"I'm a most religious fellow," Lennon said. "I was brought up a Christian and I only now understand some of the things that Christ was saying in those parables. Because people got hooked on the teacher and missed the message."[21]

One of the songs that didn't make the final cut on *Double Fantasy* was an outtake called "Help Me to Help Myself." In it, Lennon sings about being plagued by destruction—most likely self-destruction, of which he was acutely aware—but also of being close to the Lord. He knows he has always been close to God ("the leaves are shining in the sun"), that they never parted. He just asks for some help to help himself.

No question about it: John Lennon was searching for something more. Should that surprise us? He had climbed to the very top of the mountain and found there was nothing there. Very few, if any, have experienced what he and his bandmates experienced in what was dubbed "Beatlemania."

People hung on Lennon's every word, and he had a lot to say. But he would contradict himself from one sentence to another. As the Beatles were exploding, Lennon wrote an anthem that would become the title of a film and album, *Help!* Because of the upbeat and catchy sound of the song, one could easily miss the cry of a young man who was in pain and in need of answers when he wrote it.

Apparently, no one was there to help John Lennon. They just wanted him to write the next hit song.

Lennon's bandmate and writing partner, Paul McCartney, said of *Help!*: "We all felt the same way. But looking back on it, John was always looking for help. He had (a paranoia) that people died when he was around. His father left home when John was three, the uncle he lived with died later, then his mother died. I think John's whole life was a cry for help."[22]

That matches the belief Robert Rosen came to after he read and memorized Lennon's diaries:

> The story of John Lennon's life was that he was always looking for the answer. Looking for the thing that was going to stop the pain and make him feel whole. He tried all these different things to stop the original pain of his father leaving him and his mother dying, and he was never able to find it. He tried to fill the emptiness he felt inside with money and fame, and that didn't work either. . . . It's a tragic story, no question about it.[23]

An unspeakable tragedy prematurely ended John Lennon's tumultuous life: he was murdered in cold blood by a deranged so-called fan who tracked him down in New York City on December 8, 1980.

Mark David Chapman stood outside the Dakota building where John and Yoko lived, waiting for them to walk out. When they did, Chapman thrust his copy of John's new album toward the former Beatle; John was gracious enough to sign it, even asking, "Do you need anything else?"

The Lennons left for a recording session at the Record Factory and later returned to the Dakota. As they approached the building, Chapman fired five hollow-point bullets from a .38 revolver into the musical legend's back. Lennon was rushed to Roosevelt Hospital in a police car. As they were driving there, one of the officers turned back and said, "Do you know who you are?" Lennon nodded yes and groaned. Sadly, Lennon succumbed to his wounds in the hospital, despite the surgeons' frantic efforts to save him.

Those five bullets were shots heard around the world; Lennon was mourned by legions of fans on every continent. Ironically, my wife and I were in London when we heard the news; we were deeply shocked and saddened. It was such a tragic ending to a difficult life.

I have visited many people on their deathbeds over the years. When people know eternity is near, they generally want to know they can go to Heaven. I only hope that John Lennon, perhaps in the final minutes of his life, remembered the moment when he proudly proclaimed that he believed in Jesus.

The Bible tells the story of Jesus being crucified between two hardened criminals. One of them turned to Christ and said, "Lord, remember me when you come into Your Kingdom." Jesus said in response, "Truly I say to you, today you will be with Me in paradise!"

At the beginning of this book, I mentioned that there will be "three surprises when we get to Heaven. Some of the people we thought would be there, won't be. Some of the people we never thought would be there will be. And surprise number three: we will be there."

Is John Lennon in Heaven?

I don't know, but I know that God in Heaven loved him.

I know that the Lord bestowed upon him extraordinary talents.

And I know that if John Lennon called out to Jesus, even in the last moments of his life, his prayer was heard.

I sincerely hope to see him on the other side.

CHAPTER SEVEN

Dazed and Confused . . . and Redeemed

E veryone was searching in the 1970s, but they were all searching for something different. For some, it was the perfect Saturday night under a disco ball, consisting of cocaine highs and dancing in skintight, shiny trousers. For others, it was far-out enlightenment from the Hare Krishnas or the peaceful, easy feeling promised by a country rock song. Maybe, instead of saving the world, for some it was about saving the earth, the whales, and the environment, or saving the inner self through Reiki or primal scream therapy.

While the 1960s were about ending the war and creating a just society, the 1970s were about creating the ideal you. If you wanted to ditch the cigarettes and alcohol and get healthy, you read *The Complete Book of Running* and hit the pavement with Jim Fixx (who tragically died of a heart attack while out running). For another form of exercise, there was *The Joy of Sex*, complete with its awkward pen-and-ink drawings. It's gastronomic cousin, *The Joy of Cooking*, made many Americans put down the can opener and pick

93

up a chef's knife. The first gourmet food market—Balducci's—opened in New York City in 1972.

Spirituality in the 1970s was a real buffet that offered a little of everything. You could have a taste of Zen meditation and pot while listening to George Harrison's "My Sweet Lord" on your hi-fi stereo. You could go full Hindu with a guru or pick up a crystal, fire up some incense, chant the night away, and call yourself a "New Ager."

The 1970s music scene reflected the balkanization of the popular culture. If you liked soft rock, there was the Carpenters or Bread. If you wanted something harder, you listened to Led Zeppelin or Van Halen. If you wanted to expand your mind and explore the boundaries of the universe, you cranked up Pink Floyd or Yes. For middle-of-the-roaders, there were the soothing sounds of ABBA and the Bee Gees. If you liked androgynous glam, David Bowie and T. Rex checked all the boxes. If you wanted to smoke a doobie and hitchhike down a dirt road with your long hair flying in the breeze, then country rock was for you. And then there was Alice Cooper, who stood in a category all his own.

The novel excesses of rockers using drugs in the 1960s had by now almost become institutionalized. It was expected. Bands had employees whose full-time job was procuring drugs. Managers stepped in when dealers failed. Roadies kept the stashes topped off and handed out backstage passes to the most beautiful women in the crowd. Label executives kept radio deejays and records spinning with sparkling white powder purchased through the company's "petty cash" fund. The music industry was suffused with drugs.

Richie Furay of the bands Buffalo Springfield and Poco is a good friend whom I have known for many years. He experienced this firsthand. A young Richie was put to the test by rocker Gram

Parsons, who overdosed in 1973. One night, Parsons went to the freezer in his apartment and pulled out a tray of ice cubes laced with LSD. He dropped it in Richie's hands and said, "We're going to take these and get high." Riche's heart raced and his hands shook. Pot was one thing, but hallucinogens scared the heck out of him. He told Parsons he couldn't do it. Parsons simply said, "Well, smoke this (pot) and make sure we don't jump out the window."[1]

Mark Farner, a founding member of Grand Funk Railroad—a powerful trio that was one of the biggest bands of the 1970s—amassed quite a decadent rock and roll resume. He experienced overnight success, gained sudden wealth, lost fortunes, had ego clashes with bandmates, suffered derailed relationships, faced angry mobs, and endured an epic battle with the IRS that was eventually resolved. And, of course, he battled the obligatory substance abuse issues.

Hanging out backstage with Jimi Hendrix at a music festival on Randall's Island, New York, in July 1970 almost cost him his life.

"Jimi's right-hand man, a guy everyone knew as 'Rabbit,' came to my dressing room and said, 'Jimi wants to see you, man,'" Farner recalled.

> So, I go; we hug and exchange "How ya doings?" and niceties. Then I look over Jimi's shoulder and see these guys in the corner doing lines of something, and they invite me to do it with them. I said, "Oh no, I don't do that, man." Rabbit kept after me while Jimi's snorting these huge snowdrifts of lines. Rabbit takes out a knife, sticks the tip in it, and brings it up to my nose, and I say, "Okay, I'll do just a little whiff." I did, and I was so out of it that I fell on top of an equipment truck to the ground. I was scraped up by a couple of assistants and taken by limo to the hotel where I threw up all night and

experienced cold sweats. I was sick, sick, sick. Let me tell you—that was the cure. Had I taken any more than that, I probably would have died.[2]

Farner wasn't alone in that era. There were several other entertainers who had their fill of wine, women, and weed. If they weren't dying like Gram Parsons or losing their minds like others, they were simply getting tired of the merry-go-round.

By the age of thirty, most of these rockers had seen and done it all. They drank top-shelf booze in the backs of limos, chased models around guitar-shaped swimming pools behind their luxurious mansions, fed raw steak to their pet cheetahs, and snorted more powder than Johnson & Johnson sold in a month.

When these artists reached the ends of their ropes, they figured out they needed something else in their lives. Some, like George Harrison, Pete Townshend, and Carlos Santana, turned to Eastern religion while others went the self-help or New Age route. But a surprising number of them turned to Jesus Christ. Those included Farner, Furay, Al Green, Donna Summer, Bernie Leadon of the Eagles, Joe English of Wings, Bonnie Bramlett of Delaney & Bonnie, Philip Bailey of Earth, Wind & Fire, Roger McGuinn of the Byrds, Dan Peek of America, Rick Wakeman of Yes, John Schlitt of Head East, Rick Cua of Outlaws, Reggie Vinson (who played and wrote songs for Alice Cooper), Graeham Goble of the Little River Band, Kerry Livgren of Kansas, Lou Gramm of Foreigner, and Randy Cutlip, a keyboardist for Three Dog Night. Many of these artists had been raised in Christian homes and returned to their spiritual roots, or they simply opened their hearts and asked Jesus Christ to come in—to live there.

That's what Dion DiMucci did in December 1979. Known to his fans simply as Dion, he was raised in the Little Italy section of

Million Dollar Quartet: Elvis Presley, Johnny Cash, Carl Perkins, and Jerry Lee Lewis—true pioneers of rock and roll and music's "Million Dollar Quartet"—were all church-going country boys. Though they believed in Jesus, the devil seduced their souls and didn't let go for decades. However, they all eventually found their way back to the light and rolled in His glory. *(Photo by Photofest)*

The Fab Four: The Beatles changed music and popular culture with their signature sound, hairstyles, and humor with their 1964 arrival in America. Spiritually, these pied pipers led a generation down a long and winding road, and sadly, for the most part, it was the blind leading the blind, as evidenced in this photo of them with spiritual guru Maharishi Mahesh Yogi, circa 1967. *(Photo by Alamy)*

The Greatest: Jimi Hendrix could play behind his head and with his teeth, getting sounds out of his instrument no one thought possible. When he set his guitar on fire at the 1969 Newport Pop Festival, the act was without precedent. A year later, he was dead at age 27. The coroner estimated Hendrix took as many as nine sleeping pills that fateful night and determined it was mostly likely an accident. To this day, many consider him the greatest guitarist who's ever lived. *(Photo by Alamy)*

The First Female: Janis Joplin joined the 27 Club three weeks after Jimi Hendrix. The rebellious and self-destructive Texan found her voice in the church choir and a few years later transformed into America's first female rock star. She also led the rock-star lifestyle, sinking into a hunger for alcohol, narcotics, and anything bad for her body and soul. Joplin's short but impactful career inspired countless other performers, including Joan Jett, Alicia Keys, and Pink. *(Photo by Alamy)*

Icon: With his tight leather pants and hypnotic performances, the Doors lead singer Jim Morrison became a sex symbol to the young girls of the 1960s. His premature death in Paris in 1971 remains obscured by mystery, rumor, and conspiracy theories. His death certificate states he died of heart failure, but no autopsy was ever performed. *(Photo by Alamy)*

The Godfather of Christian Rock: Larry Norman penned songs, musicals, and rock operas during the day and preached on the street to businessmen, transvestites, prostitutes, and hippies at night. He did not compose songs for the church; he wrote pop and rock songs for unbelievers with messages about faith. Today, critics agree that Larry Norman is to Christian music what Bob Dylan is to modern music. *(Photo by Alamy)*

The Chameleon: Bob Dylan is known for hiding behind his Wayfarers and constantly changing his persona. He went from folk to electric rock, was the prophet of protest, and went again from Nashville crooner to circus ringleader. But in 1979, he became a very unexpected and outspoken follower of Jesus Christ. He even issued three Gospel-infused albums to prove it. Throughout his career, fans and critics alike have struggled to figure him out. *(Photo by Alamy)*

Dylan the Disciple: Bob Dylan attended a five-month course of intense Bible study with about a dozen other students under the discipleship of several Vineyard Christian Fellowship pastors in Southern California in 1979. In this photo, Dylan (far left with hand on hip) can be seen with his Vineyard classmates. *(Photo courtesy of Jennifer Goetz)*

The Intersection: Rarely do popular culture and Christianity intersect, but it happened in the early 1970s when the Jesus Movement in Southern California drove the groundswell for a national audience. Plays, movie productions, and songs got their moment in the spotlight, giving Jesus superstar status among youth and the pop culture elite—some for better, some for worse. Greg Laurie, pictured in this photo with The Way, a popular Jesus rock group, witnessed this movement up close. *(Photo courtesy of Greg Laurie)*

The Tourist: Former Beatle John Lennon visited many different spiritual traditions, never committing to any of them. He explored Transcendental Meditation with the rest of the Beatles in India and later sponsored International Society for Krishna Consciousness founder A. C. Bhaktivedanta Swami Prabhupada and a handful of Hare Krishnas at his eighty-acre English country estate. He briefly explored Christianity while his wife, Yoko Ono, turned to psychics, witchcraft, and the occult. At the end of his life, Lennon called himself a "Zen pagan." *(Photo by Alamy)*

True Believer: For decades, Richie Furay of Buffalo Springfield and Poco focused all his attention on music and fame, only to discover neither fulfilled him spiritually. When he listened to a sixty-minute sermon on tape called "The More Sure Word" by Pastor Chuck Smith of Calvary Chapel in Costa Mesa, California, it was the breakthrough he'd been looking for. Furay founded Calvary Chapel in Boulder, Colorado, in 1982; he still writes, records, and tours occasionally. *(Photo courtesy of Alamy)*

The Grandest Funk: Grand Funk Railroad's Mark Farner survived overnight success, sudden wealth, derailed relationships, angry mobs, lost fortunes, betrayal, million-dollar lawsuits, death threats, and an epic battle with the IRS before he reached the end of himself and the beginning of eternal life. *(Photo courtesy of Capitol Records)*

The Showman: The Alice Cooper Band changed rock music forever with their signature sound, surrealistic stage show, and Alice's over-the-top, horror-inspired persona. Their 1973 tour not only shattered all previous box office records but defined the modern era of touring. Alice and his band of musical brothers chugged, snorted, inhaled, imbibed, ripped, tripped, and tweaked on all the devil's candy they could lay their hands on. He is proof that God does give second, third, and fourth chances in life—amazing grace until we draw our last breath. *(Photo by Alamy)*

Shock Rock: Who'da thunk it? Dee Snider, lead singer of heavy metal band Twisted Sister was born and raised a Christian. He also doesn't drink, smoke, or do drugs. The sixty-five-year-old rocker has been married to his wife Suzette, a costume designer, since 1981. They have four children and four grandchildren. *(Photo by Alamy)*

The Antidote: C. C. DeVille was the lead guitarist for Poison, one of the most popular charting hair bands of the 1980s. But he didn't seem it enjoy it much. He was so high that much of the time he didn't know where he was. He finally called on the Lord to help him with his sobriety, and said grace is what ultimately made him change. *(Photo by Alamy)*

Megatalent, Megaproblems: As the lead guitarist in Metallica and founder of Megadeth, Dave Mustaine played like an angel, but drank like a demon and went to rehab fifteen times. In a moment of serenity, he found God. He says he doesn't believe in religion but maintains a personal relationship with Jesus Christ. *(Photo by Alamy)*

Silent Serenity: Rudy Sarzo has always lived by faith. He didn't become a Christian out of a need to be moral or because he once led a decadent lifestyle. The bassist for Ozzy Osbourne and later Quiet Riot was raised in the Catholic faith, and from a young age had his feet firmly on the ground. He faced many temptations as a rock star and turned his back on the things he knew were destructive, even if it might cost him a lucrative gig. His faith has remained steadfast. *(Photo by Alamy)*

Sk8 Prophets: Korn is an alternative rock-metal-industrial-rap-hip-hop group that emerged in the 1990s in Bakersfield, California, with a niche following of skate rats with sleeve tattoos, shaved heads, and multiple piercings, but they sold more than forty million albums—an astounding number. They also racked up an impressive eight top-five albums, forty-one singles, and two Grammy awards. Two of its members—Brian "Head" Welch and Reginald "Fieldy" Arvizu—were world-class partiers with world-class addictions; today both are Christians. Korn from left to right: James "Munky" Shaffer, Welch, Jonathan Davis, Arvizu, and Ray Luzier. *(Photo by Alamy)*

Trading Glamour for Glory: One of the most talented and energetic percussionists of the twentieth century, Sheila E. led "The Glamorous Life." But after years of touring, studio sessions, and punishing drumbeats, every part of her body ached and was sometimes paralyzed. She began attending church and reading the Scriptures regularly. She also made a personal commitment to Jesus Christ and demonstrated it by doing ministry work, making sure to be a blessing to someone or something every day of the week. *(Photo by Alamy)*

True Belieber: Justin Bieber's popularity commenced when he was just thirteen. The ride was all fun and games at first—and then Bieber, like a lot of famous people, found himself at the end of Lonely Street. The Canadian teen allowed his ego and power to take over all his relationships, and each began to suffer as a result. There was also plenty of drinking, drugs, and promiscuity. He turned to Jesus Christ when he hit rock bottom, and today is on a much better track. *(Photo by Alamy)*

Brooklyn. He was christened as a Catholic when he was a baby but didn't see the inside of a church again for decades. He began drinking at age twelve and was drugging a year later. The biggest narcotic of all—fame—came when his vocal group, Dion and the Belmonts, scored their first hit with "I Wonder Why" in 1958— Dion was just nineteen years old. Other singles followed, including early rock and roll classics "A Teenager in Love," "Runaround Sue," and "The Wanderer."

On February 3, 1959, Dion was touring with Buddy Holly, Ritchie Valens, and J. P. Richardson ("The Big Bopper") under the banner of the "Winter Dance Party." He had an opportunity to fly to their next gig in Clear Lake, Iowa, but the plane only had room for three passengers. Dion won a coin toss, but let Valens go in his place because he couldn't justify paying $36 for a flight that would take less than two hours.

"A light went off in my head because my father paid that monthly for rent in the Bronx," Dion later recalled to *Forbes* magazine writer Jim Clash. "So I thought, 'I'm not going to spend a whole month's rent just for a flight.' My primary reason for not going was the $36! So I said to Ritchie, 'Please, you go on the plane. Take your coat. Stay warm. I'll watch your guitars.'"

Tragically, the plane crashed, killing everyone on board. The tragedy sent shockwaves through the musical world and was the inspiration for Don McClean's classic, "American Pie." He describes the poignant death of Buddy Holly as "the day the music died." Holly was a major influence on many other artists, including the Beatles.

By the early 1960s Dion was a big star on a major record label, touring worldwide and appearing in a feature film called *Twist Around the Clock*. Those successes masked a big problem: Dion had struggled with heroin addiction since his teens. But that changed on April 1, 1968, when he got down on his knees and asked God to take away his obsessions with drugs and alcohol. His faith in Christ crystalized on December 14, 1979, when he got involved in a twelve-step spiritual recovery program and prayed a simple prayer.

"God, I would like to be closer to You."

Wish granted. He recalled at that very moment of having a vision of Christ, who He was, what He could do, and His place in history.

"It changed my life; I've never been the same," Dion told the *National Catholic Register* in 2011.

I became friends with Dion after he recorded a string of Christian albums in the 1980s. To this day, his voice is as clear as it was when he was in the Belmonts in the 1950s. He played at our church a few times and has been married to his wife, Susan, since 1963.

The Rock & Roll Hall of Famer has kept active musically and has influenced many of the artists who came after him. He recently recorded *Stomping Ground* (2021), an album of brand-new music with a little help from friends like Eric Clapton, Bruce Springsteen, Peter Frampton, Rickie Lee Jones, and a host of others.

• • •

Though some see rock and roll as the antithesis of religion, the truth is, many rock stars have become people of faith because they've lived at the pinnacle of a pagan world and know that ultimately, it's not satisfying. It shouldn't be terribly shocking that when someone has "been there, done that, and bought the T-shirt," they would search for more. Many of these bands literally were on the T-shirts.

God used Elvis Presley's death in August 1977 to call the Byrds lead singer Roger McGuinn, who grew up Catholic, to repentance.

The Byrds were one of the biggest bands of the mid-to-late '60s and early '70s—so big that they strongly influenced the Beatles. They were best known for McGuinn's trademark shades, his jangly Rickenbacker guitar, and the blending voices of McGuinn, Gene Clark, David Crosby, and Chris Hillman.

McGuinn said, "(Elvis) was only seven years older and died at forty-two. I was thirty-five at the time and using all the same drugs. I had a pill doctor in LA who would give me anything I wanted. I decided I had better change my lifestyle. As I gradually got rid of the bad things, the Lord had better access to my spirit."[3]

The change came when McGuinn prayed with a piano player named Billy.

"I never knew his last name. I told him my symptoms and he asked, 'Do you believe in the power of prayer?'" McGuinn recalled. "I said, 'Yes,' so he held my hands and said a simple prayer. 'Oh Lord Jesus, come into this man's heart in Your own time, in Jesus's name.'"[4]

McGuinn has been a committed Christian for more than four decades now. In fact, he and his wife share an active prayer and devotional life, including Bible study for an hour or two every morning. The man who sang, "Turn! Turn! Turn!" finally embraced his own advice.

Chris Hillman was McGuinn's bandmate in the Byrds and grew up in an interfaith home—Jewish and Presbyterian. His mother's cousin was a minister at a church about seven miles from their California home. Hillman loved hymns as a child. When he was in sixth grade, rock and roll exploded with Elvis Presley, but that didn't make young Hillman want to learn guitar; folk music did that when it came along a few years later. In 1964, when the Beatles invaded our shores, he traded his guitar for an electric bass and joined the Byrds.

Things took a darker turn for Hillman in the 1970s. He witnessed the deaths of friends Gram Parsons and Clarence White of the Kentucky Colonels and saw firsthand how the drug scene took many musicians to their early graves. The ones who did come out alive were lost in a repeat cycle of never-ending spinning. In a moment of doubt and fear in 1979, Hillman reached out to Jesus while in a plummeting airplane.

"I was feeling helpless and scared as the plane bounced around," Hillman wrote in his 2020 memoir, *Time Between*. "On that flight I reached out to God . . . and I prayed and accepted Jesus Christ into my life." He promised to follow Him for the rest of his life. But when the plane landed safely, he walked away from his promise.

"I may have abandoned God the next morning, but God never abandoned me," Hillman said.[5]

He certainly didn't. Jesus waited patiently for Hillman to come back around. That finally happened in 1980.

"I was by myself, and I just heard The Voice," he said. "I just broke down into tears. I don't know what triggered it, but something did something to me and that was it. And I accepted Him, truly accepted Him, this time."[6]

. . .

For Richie Furay, salvation didn't come at the end of a harrowing plane ride or a voice coming from Heaven: it was the threat of his wife leaving him. Furay's vice wasn't drugs or drink, but fidelity. He had taken up with a mistress while on tour.

"When you're on the road for so long, you don't know what's real and what isn't," Furay said. "It was very hard at that time because I was so driven to be a rock and roll star. I had seen Stephen Stills and Neil Young go off to great success. I had seen Jimmy

Messina and Randy Meisner do the same . . . I was so consumed and driven to succeed that I had no grasp on reality."[7]

But soon, reality would come crashing down on him. When the tour ended, Furay's wife Nancy told him she wanted a divorce. Richie was startled that Nancy was so quick to move on with her life. He went back on tour and, a few weeks later, was hit by the Holy Spirit in the Lone Star State.

"We were in Texas when the scales fell from my eyes," he recalled. "In a moment I realized I was making the worst mistake of my life. I was terrified and felt sick inside. I had no explanation for the way this feeling came over me, but I know it was the Holy Spirit stepping into my life."[8]

The Holy Spirit not only stepped into Furay's life, He took it over. But life wasn't a bed of roses after his conversion.

That was when I met Richie. I remember how heartbroken and devastated he was without Nancy in his life. It took more spiritual revelations and more hardship and pain before she accepted him again.

Furay went on to a solo career in which he sang of his new-found faith with the Richie Furay Band. His 1976 album, *I've Got a Reason*, was one of the best of the decade, though it was overlooked by many. Richie went on to found Calvary Chapel in Boulder, Colorado, in 1982. He still writes, records, and tours occasionally. Amazingly, his voice is as strong as ever. When he reunited with his bandmates Stephen Stills and Neil Young for a Buffalo Springfield tour in 2010, Young introduced Richie as the lead singer of the band—quite a compliment.

My son Jonathan and I had the opportunity to see them play a reunion show in LA in 2010, and it was nothing short of amazing. Richie also officiated the wedding of my other son, Christopher, in Hawaii in 2006.

In "I've Got a Reason," he sang, "Music was my life, finally took everything." Richie later said of his rough spiritual patch and ultimate redemption: "Looking back, I can see the Lord never takes anything away that he doesn't replace with something that's far greater. I had thought music was what it was all about for me, but I was quickly learning that for life to have real meaning, Jesus has to be the foundation; everything else must be built upon Him!"[9]

I have jokingly told Nancy Furay that she has had more love songs written about her than any other woman on earth. Fact is, throughout his esteemed career, Richie has sung exclusively about one woman! That must be a first in the annals of rock history.

• • •

Another hugely successful rock band of the 1970s was Foreigner. They had hit after hit from "Feels Like the First Time" to "Hot Blooded" to "Juke Box Hero" and the monster smash, "I Wanna Know What Love Is."

Lead singer Lou Gramm has one of the greatest voices in rock music—but that didn't keep him from going down the predictable rabbit hole of rock excess. During Foreigner's heyday in the late 1970s and early 1980s, drugs were a natural part of the scene—but they were changing Lou for the worse, and he knew it. Life on the road, partying late into the night, and not getting enough sleep started to fray his nerves. He said that in the late 1980s through the early 1990s, he was doing some "spiritual shopping."

One night in a hotel room, he had a revelation of how this would all end for him.

"I saw the possibility of my own demise," he later told Scott Ross of CBN. "It was in this huge, posh hotel room that I got down on my knees asking for God's help to heal me and help me to rid myself of this horrible addiction. I just started praying because I knew there wasn't anybody in the world that could help me."[10]

Ross asked him if he had asked Jesus Christ to come into his life.

"I definitely did it because that's what I wanted for a long time, and it was an option that He was offering to me," Gramm said.[11]

I came to know Lou personally when we did an event in Rochester, New York, where he lived at the time. Lou is a down-to-earth, humble guy, especially considering his massive success. He even sang a version of "I Wanna Know What Love Is" at our event, changing the lyrics to reflect his newfound faith.

• • •

By the end of the 1970s, Kansas was one of the top-grossing acts in the world and creatively at the top of their game. That was due mostly to the talents of Kerry Livgren, whose contemplative lyrics and thoughtful sonic waves created a unique rock sound dug by millions.

A popular text among those who did drugs was *The Urantia Book*, a dog's breakfast of spiritualism, philosophy, and religion. No one knows who wrote it or even exactly when it was published (though the year 1955 has been proffered). Another mystery is exactly what it's about. It claims to be presented by aliens and touches on topics such as the origin and meaning of life, the life of Jesus, and mankind's place in the universe. In other words, it's a flaky mishmash that no one really takes seriously.

But Livgren did—for the better part of a year.

Livgren grew up in a Christian household but veered away from that teaching and truth and embraced Buddhism for a time. He was a voracious reader who knew a little something about every religion but, oddly enough, never actually studied the Bible. In July 1979, he had been touring with the band and promoting their latest album, *Monolith*. Their opening act was a band from Louisiana called Le Roux (best known for the song "Nobody Said It Was Easy"). Between shows, Livgren rode in the back of the tour bus with vocalist Jeff Pollard, arguing about whether the Bible or *The Urantia Book* was the most accurate record of Jesus's life. Pollard convinced Livgren that the Bible was the genuine record, and Livgren surrendered his life to God accordingly.

"The world is speeding to a very obvious conclusion," Livgren told a reporter shortly after his conversion. "As that transpires, more and more people are realizing that Christ is the answer and coming forward. It's just not rock musicians—we just happen to be more in the public eye, and it's more newsworthy because rock is considered to be so decadent."[12]

Livgren started taking a lesser role with Kansas after he became a Christian, which almost coincided with the advent of MTV. Executives by then were focused on video-friendly singles, and songs like "Carry on Wayward Son" and "Dust in the Wind" just weren't going to cut it any longer. Livgren eventually left Kansas in 1985 to form AD, a Christian rock band. He had a stroke in 2009 but recovered.

That is around the time I came to know him personally. Our church had booked AD to play one night, and I asked them to perform "Carry on Wayward Son." They obliged—and promptly blew out our sound system. That was a first. But that's what happens when you invite a top-shelf rock band to play through a system that's not designed to accommodate what they do. It was an epic night.

These days, Kerry works on various musical projects. He still records, sometimes guest-stars with Kansas at various concerts, and was the caregiver for his wife, Victoria, when she had breast cancer a few years ago (she was cleared in 2018). He continues to read the Bible and regularly attends church with his family. He also has advice for all his fans:

"May you all find the miracles in your own lives. Look for them, for they are surely there, and especially the greatest miracle of all—God's love and provision for mankind."[13]

• • •

It took a few years for Mark Farner to find the miracle in his life. Grand Funk Railroad, a garage band from Flint, Michigan, rose to global superstardom within the span of a year. They charted nineteen singles—two of which were number ones—and accumulated thirteen gold and ten platinum records that sold more than twenty-five million copies worldwide.

But tensions brewed within the group for several years as the hits, misses, financial mismanagement, and continual pressure of working nonstop on the road and in the studio (delivering two albums a year) caused artistic stagnation and eventual burnout. The band broke up in late 1976, and Farner spent the next seven years boozing, smoking pot with his buddies, and coming and going as he pleased, despite having a wife and two sons. One day, he came home to find a note from his wife, Lesia, saying that said she'd left.

"It flattened me," Farner said. "A week went by, and I knew she wasn't coming back."

Not long afterward, Farner was sitting at the dining room table, consuming a six-pack of beer and smoking a joint while watching his two sons playing in the living room. They kept asking for their mommy. What was he going to do?

Farner looked over at a stained-glass window in the corner of the room. A ray of light hit him square in the face and revealed a vision.

"This quick flash went off and I saw myself on my knees as a nine-year-old boy in front of that television set, praying along with Billy Graham to heal my heart because my father had just died," he later recalled. "I knew then that I needed to find God again."[14]

Farner's Christian journey never involved a dramatic, burning bush-style conversion. It was a series of small, incremental changes and choices he made over the following years, including finding a good home church. He reconciled with Lesia, got sober, and devoted more and more time to God. Eventually, he came full circle to the faith he had known as a child when he found a church in Onaway, Michigan, in September 1983.

"God placed me there that day to hear the message from this eighty-year-old pastor, who spoke on 'Marriage According to God's Law,'" Farner recalled. "The message was about how people walk out on the commitment of marriage too easily, without realizing that matrimony is holy to the Lord. His words were like six live rounds to my heart, and God doesn't use blanks. I felt this pastor was singling me out and knew my whole life story. When he gave the altar call at the end of his sermon to get saved, I didn't just walk, man. I ran!"[15]

. . .

Disco diva Donna Summer, who launched her Grammy Award-winning career with the lascivious "Love to Love You Baby" in 1975, was raised in a devout Christian home. Her father was the pastor of a church; Summer said God first spoke to her when she was ten years old. She had just finished singing a solo in the choir when she heard an inner voice.

"It sort of knocked everybody out of the pews. When I looked up through my tears, everyone in the whole church's eyes were downcast and they were crying, and I thought, 'Oh my God.' I looked at my dad and he was crying," she recalled in the final years of her life. "It was that, on that first time I ever sang, that I heard God speak to me, and He said to me that I was gonna be famous, and that I was not to misuse the power that He was giving me."[16]

"Famous" doesn't even begin to describe Summer's stratospheric rise to popularity. Her sensual mezzo-soprano voice, slew of disco hits, and unparalleled ability to get people on the dance floor made her an icon. But with fame came temptation, aggravation, and insecurity.

Summer developed a very heavy dependence on antidepressants and sleeping pills because of the demands of her white-hot career. She also became embroiled in a $10 million lawsuit with Casablanca Records owner Neil Bogart. Bogart countersued for even more money, citing breach of contract. Summer was a bundle of nerves and breaking down from the inside. She developed stomach ulcers and would barely touch her food. She had occasional thoughts of suicide despite appearing to the world that she was on top.

Summer returned to her roots of faith in 1979 after a period of "spiritual darkness and confusion." She recommitted her life to Christ and yielded to God's will. Instantly, she experienced a sense of elation and relief.

"I was finally filled by God's Holy Spirit and gloriously born again," she later reflected.[17]

The change in Summer was almost instant. She began attending a weekly Bible study and stopped performing "Love to Love You

Baby" and "Bad Girls" at the peak of her fame. She also made a point of announcing that her next album (*The Wanderer*) was going to be "spiritually inspired, but not overtly gospel."

As Summer explained:

> I never stopped being a Christian. Being born-again is an affirmation that the person is going to make a personal effort to walk closer to God and bring Him into one's life and start following His way. There are parts in your life where you can look back and laugh: "I can't believe I did that; how could I have said that; where's my head at?" I'm sad that all the running I did was only running; it didn't get me anywhere. The spirit of rebellion in myself and in my songs would not let me rest. But I've chosen to stay in the world's eye, to give a positive image. It's a very spiritual and a very helpful place to be. I love it.[18]

I spoke at a Bible study some years ago in Beverly Hills where Donna was present. Her face was beaming, and I could see she had a genuine faith in Christ. Not long after that, I was rallying people for a huge Harvest Crusade at Dodger Stadium. I was trying to make my way over to Donna afterward to have a conversation with her, but some person kept bending my ear, and I could not break free. She left shortly thereafter. I always regretted not being able to speak with her.

In what was to be her final album, *Crayons* (2008), Donna sang passionately about her faith in the song "Bring Down the Reign." She went to be with the Lord in 2012.

These '70s rockers all learned the same lesson in the end, but they came to the answer through vastly different journeys. Some of them lost their stardom, some almost lost their lives, wives, or families, while others were fortunate enough to go down smoother roads. But in the end, they all realized that, through repentance and humility, God had a special song for them, if they were just willing to listen.

At some point in that decadent decade, they were all dazed and confused. And now they are all redeemed.

CHAPTER EIGHT

Alice Unchained

Quick: what do you think of when I say the name "Alice Cooper"? The guy with a woman's name wearing extreme eye makeup? The rocker who killed a chicken on stage during a concert? (Or did he bite the head off a bat?) Rock and roll's boogeyman? A guy who belts out loud music with a huge boa constrictor draped around his neck? The godfather of shock rock? A cultural icon?

Would it surprise you to learn that this Rock & Roll Hall of Famer is a Christian? Let me correct myself: he's a shameless, outspoken, and strong Christian. He is also a nice and down-to-earth person.

I first met him in January 2019. I was preaching my usual Sunday sermon at the Orange County campus of Harvest Fellowship when I spotted a recognizable couple sitting in the front row. Alice and Sheryl Cooper had never attended Harvest before, but I knew who they were. I had known that they would be coming that day, and they knew I knew they were coming.

Alice, of course, is the Rock & Roll Hall of Famer, and Sheryl, a former professional dancer, has been his wife for forty-five years.

My friend Gabe Velasquez had attended an Alice Cooper concert in Anaheim the night before and even managed to get backstage and speak to the showman. Alice mentioned that he and Sheryl liked to attend church whenever they were on the road, and they were looking for a place to worship. Discussing convenient places of worship is not typical conversation backstage at a rock concert, but that tells you a lot about Alice. Gabe extended the offer to go to Harvest the following morning, and the Coopers showed up. No entourage. No bodyguards. No reptiles. No black makeup or eyeliner for Alice. No top hat or cane, either. No pretenses—just the two of them. They sat on the front row over to the side, and no one bothered them. After the service, they came upstairs to my office to visit with Cathe and me.

My office is probably unlike any you have ever seen, especially for a pastor.

It's sort of a man-cave-meets-serious-library situation. Over my desk is a large photo of the Beatles that my son Christopher gave me. I have an original *Help!* poster and a Sting-Ray Orange Krate bicycle, like the one I used to ride as a boy, hanging from my ceiling. I have some surfboards mounted on the walls and a few guitars, including a replica of the Rickenbacker John Lennon played on *The Ed Sullivan Show*. I also have a poster of Billy Graham from the late 1940s and busts of evangelists D. L. Moody and C. H. Spurgeon. Throw in some Disney memorabilia and a few hundred books, mainly commentaries on the books of the Bible, and you have a snapshot of my office.

When Alice walked in, he looked around, and the stories started coming:

When agent Shep Gordon was courting Alice as a client, he invited him to a hotel room filled with smoke, and there in the flesh were Jimi Hendrix, Jim Morrison, and Janis Joplin. Alice was impressed and signed with Shep immediately. Shep Gordon is still his agent a half-century later.

We found the Coopers to be extremely open and easy to talk to. So cool, so warm, and so friendly. Funny too. We are all about the same age, have the same cultural touchstones, and grew up liking many of the same things, including classic rock, guitars, and the faith that sustains us. I even discovered that as kids, Alice and I both loved to read comic books and the satirical magazine, *MAD*.

But the thing we liked to talk about the most was Jesus. Alice knows his Bible, and he openly talks about what Jesus means to him. Alice is featured doing this in a documentary coming out this year that we produced with the Kingdom Story Company titled *FAME*.

If you've never seen an Alice Cooper concert, let me just tell you that no one ever gets cheated. The energy he expends on stage is that of a man thirty years his junior, and when on tour, he does it five nights a week. The fact that he got up in the morning to go to church astounded me. Our visit flew by, and at the end, we vowed to stay in touch.

A few months later, I emailed Alice to ask if he'd be open to videotaping a wide-ranging conversation, which ended up almost mimicking the one we had that day in my office. I figured if we could get that on tape, we'd be gold.

Alice said he'd be happy to oblige if I flew to Phoenix, where he and Sheryl have lived since the 1980s. We arranged for our interview to take place at his nonprofit foundation, one of the two locations of Alice Cooper's Solid Rock Teen Center. The complex, which is the Coopers' gift to the community, inspires and challenges teens to embrace excellence and reach their full potential. Solid Rock offers free training in music, dance, sound and recording engineering, lighting, staging, video production, and art, and provides a computer lab in a cool, supervised facility where the teens can engage with their peers. At the start of the interview, Alice spoke about why he opened Solid Rock.

"I watched a couple of sixteen-year-old kids do a drug deal on the corner. I went, 'How does that kid not know he might be a great guitar player? Or that that other kid might be a drummer?'" he said. "And it just struck me right then. Why don't we give them an alternative?"[1]

The center took millions to launch in 1995, not to mention lots of elbow grease and hours upon hours of planning—and it's totally free to the teens who walk through the doors. You wouldn't blame them if they wondered if there's a catch or why Alice Cooper, who could be working on his golf handicap, does this.

"We're all a bunch of Christian guys here, and the Lord told us to do it, so we just obeyed," he said with great humility. "So that's all."[2]

That's all?

Alice's commitment to help others and his willingness to submit to the Lord is so simple, yet inspiring. This place has become precious to him, and I can see why. He's offering a haven for young people, a place where they might develop a hidden talent. He wants to expand to more locations in the Phoenix metro area and throughout the state in places like Tucson, Casa Grande, and Flagstaff. It's not unlike "seeding" a startup church.

You may be surprised to hear this, but Alice's roots are in the church. His grandfather was an evangelist, and his father was a part-time pastor. Alice grew up knowing who the Lord was, but when he discovered Elvis Presley, the Beatles, and rock and roll, it took his focus away from Christ.

Vincent Damon Furnier was born on February 4, 1948, at Saratoga Hospital in Detroit. The hospital was located on the east side of the city, just south of the infamous 8 Mile Road. Cooper said its nickname was "Butcher's Palace: because not everyone came out in one piece." However, he fared well compared to some of the other infants.

He was born with eczema and infantile asthma. He overcame the first ailment, but the second required a move to a more climate-friendly place, so his parents pulled up stakes and moved to California's San Fernando Valley. There his father, Ether Moroni Furnier (known as "Mick"), found work as an engineer at the Jet Propulsion Laboratory in Pasadena while his mother, Ella, took a job waitressing at Lawry's on La Cienega Boulevard in LA. Young Vince spent a lot of his free time at a movie theater that showed eight consecutive hours of horror movies every Saturday.

When Vince became "Alice Cooper" (the name evolved from a three-week brainstorming session), his act looked like a horror movie with writhing snakes, electric chairs, fake blood, cut-up doll toys, and—best of all—having his own head cut off by a guillotine at the end of the show. It was all an act, of course, but it entertained his audience of young people and outraged their parents. Mission accomplished.

After moving to Los Angeles, his parents began attending church and deepening their faith. It changed all the Furniers' lives, but especially Mick's. He gave up his three-pack-a-day smoking habit, cleared out the liquor cabinet, and cleaned up his language. The family was in church every Sunday, Wednesday, and Friday. On Saturdays, they cleaned the church for the next day's services.

"The church was suddenly everything to us—a religion, a social life, a new family," Alice said. "My father's devotion was inspiring. It affected my mother so deeply that within a month, she stood up in church one day and asked to be baptized. My father did the same thing a few weeks later, and after that, our lives changed completely."[3]

Mick Furnier was ordained in 1961 when Vince was thirteen. That was the same year the family moved to Arizona—and the same year, Vince almost lost his life. Two months after moving to Phoenix, he got violently ill after eating lasagna; the family concluded that his stomach couldn't handle spicy foods. But later, his parents found him passed out in a pool of vomit in his bedroom and rushed him to the hospital.

Doctors opened him up and discovered his insides were riddled with peritonitis. His appendix had burst a few days earlier, and every internal organ had been affected. The doctors extracted four quarts of poison from Vince's system, then sewed him up, inserted drainage tubes, and pumped him full of morphine. They also told Mick and Ella their son had a 10 percent chance of survival and to prepare themselves for the worst. The Furniers instinctively put on their spiritual armor and went to battle for young Vince in prayer.

"My parents sat by my bedside and read the Bible and comic books to me: 'The sickness is not unto death but unto the glory of God.' I looked like I was ready for Hitler's ovens," Alice said later of dropping almost half his weight.

> I reached a low of sixty-eight pounds. A call for help went out to church members and believers around the country. In Los Angeles, the church people who ordained my dad prayed and fasted for me. Letters and cards arrived to the hospital by the dozens while my parents

waited for the end to come. I can't offer any explanation as to why I lived except that it was a miracle. There is no doubt about it. It was a miracle that I pulled through, thanks to Jesus and the church and the faith of everyone around me.

Years later, whenever my father would tell this story to people they'd laugh. Why would the Lord save the life of Alice Cooper?[4]

The answer to that question would not be revealed for a few decades.

In 1964, a few years after his bout with peritonitis, Vince had an ordination of his own when a quartet from Liverpool appeared on *The Ed Sullivan Show*. Vince, along with seventy-three million other Americans, tuned in to watch these four "mop-tops" perform their incredibly catchy songs, which made young girls instinctively lose their minds. And it changed his life.

"The Beatles were like from another planet with the long hair and strange accents, but they were funny," Alice said. "They had a great sense of humor. The girls loved them, which immediately got our attention."[5]

I've heard literally thousands of other musicians express the same sentiment over the years—that the Beatles inspired them to pick up an instrument and play music for a living. As a lifelong fan, I have developed a deep understanding of musicians and artists, and totally respect their passion, dedication, and the hours they spend on their craft.

The 1960s was truly a special decade for music. In addition to the Beatles, on any given day, the radio blasted artists like Bob Dylan, the Rolling Stones, the Beach Boys, Led Zeppelin, the Who, the Byrds, Jimi Hendrix, Cream, the Doors, Janis Joplin, Sly & the

Family Stone, Jefferson Airplane—and that's without even mentioning Motown Records, which gave us artists like Aretha Franklin, Diana Ross and the Supremes, Marvin Gaye, Stevie Wonder, the Temptations, Smokey Robinson, and the Jackson 5. The music was fun, uplifting, challenging, psychedelic, and dramatic. It was truly a soundtrack to a generation.

By that time, Vince was a class clown and jock who ran track at Apollo High School, which then was at the northern edge of Phoenix. He was also a gifted mimic who could imitate Barney Fife, Inspector Clouseau, or Stan Laurel with ease. He had a natural magnetism that easily drew people to him.

"I went out of my way to be charming and funny in the classroom," he said. "Not wise-guy funny, but nice funny. And I was known as a great diplomat. I could talk my way out of any fight, and I could talk my way out of just about any situation that came up."[6]

That was a notion seconded by his best friend and fellow bandmate, Dennis Dunaway. He said Vince could talk to anyone about any topic, quickly figure out what the other person wanted to hear, and then say it. He had an unlimited repertoire of tales—some of them tall, according to Dunaway. He said Vince was smart, witty, hip, and quick to laugh, especially at himself. Art class is where the two teens bonded and ultimately decided to become rock stars.

The Beatles inspired them to take that first step, and that decision was later solidified by Chuck Berry, Duane Eddy, and the Rolling Stones. But it was the Yardbirds that really put their musical imprimatur on Vince and the classic lineup of the Alice Cooper Band. (A good choice, I might add.)

The Yardbirds are one of the most overlooked bands of the 1960s. From that band alone came three of the greatest rock guitarists of all time, including Eric Clapton, Jimmy Page, and Jeff Beck. They had hits that you might recognize, including "For

Your Love" and "Heart Full of Soul." They were innovative and ahead of their time.

So was the Alice Cooper Band, which was its official name starting in April 1968. It included Dennis Dunaway on bass, Michael Bruce and Glen Buxton on guitar, and Neal Smith on drums. Between 1969 and 1973, the band released seven studio albums and a string of hits (including "Eighteen," "School's Out," "Billion Dollar Babies," and "No More Mr. Nice Guy") that changed rock music forever through a signature sound paired with a theatrical, surrealistic stage show and Alice's over-the-top, horror-inspired persona.

Critics tend to give credit to the Rolling Stones, Led Zeppelin, the Who, Three Dog Night, or the Bee Gees for being the biggest bands of the 1970s, but they should include the Alice Cooper Band in that list. Its 1973 *Billion Dollar Babies* tour not only shattered all box-office records previously held by the Rolling Stones, it also defined the modern era of touring.

The band now inhabited a world of jets, limousines, and champagne, and Alice and his musical brothers chugged, snorted, inhaled, imbibed, ripped, tripped, and tweaked on all the devil's candy they could lay their hands on. And since they were a stadium act that traveled by jet, that was a *lot*. All the while, Alice's popularity continued to shoot through the stratosphere, especially after "The Chicken."

"The Chicken" is one of rock's most memorable moments. It's right up with Hendrix setting his instrument on fire, Pete Townshend smashing his guitar, and Ozzy Osbourne biting the head off a bat. During the band's performance at the Toronto Pop Festival in June 1969, a fan tossed a live chicken on stage. Alice saw it and tossed it back into the audience. *It's a bird*, he thought at the time. *It'll fly away*. It did not; the fans tore it to shreds.

However, the rumor that made rounds was that Alice ripped the chicken's head off and drank its blood. Alice never denied it—the story was too juicy and did wonders for his street cred.

But exactly why was Alice Cooper so popular? He wasn't exactly everybody's cup of tea, especially in mainstream America. He and the band zigged when everybody else zagged. He was different and not always likeable. And that was just fine by him.

"Rock was looking for a villain, and I was more than happy to be Captain Hook to everybody's Peter Pan," Alice told me in our conversation at Solid Rock.[7]

And it worked like a charm. Alice said once the band had a hit (they had fourteen Top Ten singles and a slew of gold and platinum albums), it was "a Willy Wonka golden ticket" to everywhere, especially Hollywood. Groucho Marx went to a show and deemed that Alice's live act was simply an updated version of vaudeville. That was his entrée to the Friars Club of Beverly Hills, where all the comedians and entertainers he had loved and adored as a kid accepted him into their tight-knit world.

"I was the only rock star allowed into the Friars Club," Alice said in amazement. "There was Sinatra over there, and there was Dean Martin and Jerry Lewis over there . . . Bob Hope, Milton Berle, Steve Allen, Jimmy Durante, Sid Caesar, Johnny Carson, Sammy Davis, Jr., and all the great comedians that I adored. They're all wearing black tuxedos and I'm in black leather. They just totally accepted me. 'Hey, Coop, how are you?'"[8]

Alice appeared on talk shows and hung out with big celebrities, old and new. He even hosted *The Muppet Show*. Elvis invited him to Las Vegas, he went to New York's Studio 54 with Salvador Dali, he hung out with Andy Warhol at The Factory . . . and since hanging out with Frank Sinatra and Dean Martin somehow wasn't enough, he formed the Hollywood Vampires, a celebrity last-man-standing drinking group comprised of Ringo Starr, Keith Moon, Harry Nillson, Bernie Taupin, and Micky Dolenz. (When John Lennon was on his "Lost Weekend" in LA, he was deemed an honorary member, though he didn't do much standing.) Alice was mostly wobbly-kneed around these world-class carousers who occupied a loft inside the Rainbow Bar & Grill on the Sunset Strip.

How'd they get that unforgettable nickname?

"People started calling us the Hollywood Vampires because we'd never see daylight," Alice recalled. "We figured instead of drinking the blood of the vein, we were drinking the blood of the vine."[9]

Alice Cooper had transcended the role of rock star to infiltrate American popular culture in music, movies, television, art, and the party scene. But behind the scenes, not everything was as it appeared to be.

Alice was unraveling.

It started with beer. Alice drank it like the rock star he was. Lots of it. It even became a prop of sorts. At his alcoholic peak, he estimates he drank a case a day. That's a lot for a guy who barely weighed 140 pounds, if that.

He laughed it off, telling a reporter in 1973 that he started drinking before breakfast and kept at it all day.

"Beer puts you in a good state of mind," he said. "You don't get drunk on beer, just sort of permanently high."[10]

A few years later, beer wasn't cutting it any longer, so he graduated to whiskey and cocaine . . . then crack.

Alice had plenty of cautionary tales to show him not to go down that rock and roll highway. He had personally known Brian Jones, Jimi Hendrix, Janis Joplin, and Jim Morrison. Alice outdid them all in terms of abuse, which is saying a lot. That's an all-star list of heavy hitters.

But no one on earth can sustain that level of use forever. The first sign of the end came when Alice started vomiting blood every morning.

His doctor said that if he stopped drinking, he could probably record twenty more albums. But if he didn't, in two weeks he'd be jamming with Morrison and Hendrix in the afterlife.

"I didn't realize that I was an alcoholic until I realized that the alcohol was not fun for anyone," Alice said. "It was medicine."[11]

The rocker checked into a sanatorium in New York. It was not a six-figure country-club rehab center with handholding, day spa privileges, shopping trips, or horse therapy, either. Those kinds of places didn't exist in 1977. If you wanted to go high-end, you could head to a Swiss sanatorium, but they weren't luxurious either back then. This was a place where the patients were often people who shook uncontrollably unless they had a whiskey first thing in the morning. Wet brain—a disorder related to an acute vitamin deficiency—was common. It's a predictable complication of long-term heavy drinking combined with poor nutrition. If you live on a daily diet of Jack Daniels, Winstons, and cocaine, and eat pancakes once every three or four days, you're going to get it. Wet brain can lead to irreversible confusion, difficulty with muscle coordination, and even hallucinations. That's who Alice spent three months with at the end of 1977.

He got clean and sober, but it didn't last long, thanks to freebase cocaine appearing on the scene. That's pure cocaine, and there's never enough because it's so addictive. Scratching the carpet at four in the morning in search of that rock you're sure bounced off the mirror is a reliable sign you're off the rails. Whatever doesn't kill you makes you sleep until three in the afternoon. Many artists who freebased went off the deep end for a few years—Alice included.

Starting in the 1980s, he recorded a string of what he called "blackout albums" that ranged from rock to synth-laden new wave to hard-nosed punk. Alice didn't remember writing these "trippy songs," recording them, touring for them, or even how he made it out of bed most afternoons, despite the fact he had a loving and supportive wife in Sheryl and a newborn daughter, Calico, to live for. He was skeletal and pale, having lost a lot of weight from not eating or sleeping. The coke also aged him significantly.

Years later, he described his emaciated appearance as that of a "soldier of fortune that's on meth and he's capable of killing anybody."[12] Except the only person Alice was killing was himself.

In the fall of 1983, his family checked him into the hospital, where he was diagnosed with cirrhosis of the liver. During his two-and-a-half-week stay, he was nursed back to health on a steady diet of vitamins and nutritious food. But a lot of damage had already been done to both his body and his marriage.

Sheryl said she could no longer watch him commit slow-motion suicide and moved out of their LA residence with Calico to Chicago, Illinois, where her parents lived, as her father was then senior pastor of First Baptist Church in Oak Park. She filed for divorce in 1983. Alice said it was the lowest point of his life, but the cocaine was speaking a lot more loudly than Sheryl by that point. One morning, shortly after Sheryl and Calico left, he crawled out of bed and looked in the mirror. He was horrified by what he saw.

"It looked like my makeup, but it was blood coming down (my face)," Alice told me. "I went to the bathroom and flushed the rock down the toilet and went to bed for three days. I woke up and called her and said, 'It's done.' She said, 'You have to prove it.' And that was the beginning of our relationship coming back."[13]

It was also the beginning of his relationship with Christ coming back. As the son of a pastor and grandson of an evangelist, Alice knew who the Lord was. He'd simply been distracted by everything that had happened since he formed his band in his teens. Now, like the prodigal son, he was ready to come home.

One of the provisions for the couple getting back together in mid-1984 was that the Coopers start going to church. They moved to Arizona and attended a large church in North Phoenix that had six thousand members.

The prodigal son had returned home and allowed himself to be embraced by his fast-approaching Father once again.

"I got to a point where I was tired of this life. I knew who Jesus Christ was, and I was denying Him because I was living my own life and I was living my life without Him," Alice said. "I knew there had to come a point where I either accepted Christ and started living that life—or, if I died in this world, I was in a lot of trouble. And that's what really motivated me . . . when the Lord opens your eyes and you suddenly realize who you are and who He is, it's a whole different world."[14]

Alice's next step of faith was getting baptized. He felt like a new creature in Christ and wanted to put "Alice" to rest once and for all. His pastor, a very wise man, didn't think that was such a good idea.

"I went to my pastor and said, 'I think I got to quit being Alice Cooper,'" he recalled. "And my pastor goes, 'Really? You think God makes mistakes? Look, He put you in the exact camp of the Philistines now. So what if you're 'Alice Cooper' now? What if you're following Christ *and* you're a rock star, but you don't live the rock-star life? Your lifestyle is now your testimony.' And that made total sense to me, you know?"[15]

The newly-sober rock star had a son in 1985 (Dash) and a second daughter (Sonora) in 1992. His family expanded once again in 2012 when he opened the doors to the original Solid Rock Teen

Center in Phoenix. Built in partnership with Genesis Church, the center was fully functional after more than a decade of detailed planning and fundraising. In 2021, he opened a second center in Mesa, Arizona, in partnership with Mesa Public Schools.

Almost thirty years after surrendering his life to Christ, Alice said dealing with Alice Cooper is no longer an issue, nor is it the top priority in his life.

"You take care of your relationship with God first, then you heal your relationship with your wife, certainly your kids. And now Solid Rock is like a very big part of my life. Alice Cooper is somewhere like five or six in terms of importance," he said. "To me, the funniest and oddest thing is this character that I used to be, they used to tear (his) albums up on *The 700 Club*. Now he's an agent for Christ. And what a miracle that is! . . . I'm still playing this dark character, but he's now an agent of Christ. Yeah, very weird."[16]

It's not weird to me. I've seen many times how God can take anyone who is willing to submit to Him and transform them into a messenger of grace and hope. He can and does work miracles in people's lives all the time. Heaven is not going to be filled with perfect people, just forgiven people. We simply must admit our sin and turn from our old ways. The Bible even says, "If we confess our sin to Him, He is faithful and just to forgive our sins and to cleanse us from all wickedness" (1 John 1:9 NLT).

God does give second, third, and fourth chances in life—amazing grace until we draw our last breath. Alice embodies this. He out-partied Jim Morrison, Janis Joplin, and Jimi Hendrix. (That's worthy of some sort of twisted Grammy Award.) He's played in front of millions of people. He was one of the top rock stars in the world at a time when rock stars were emperors with private jets and albums that sold in the multimillions. But in the end, he was humbled and alone, utterly naked before God like the day he was born. And God told Alice He wasn't done with him yet. There was work for him to do. He sent the skinny rocker from Phoenix to do His will—and openly give the glory to the God who literally saved both his life and his soul.

God really does work in ways mysterious—to us.

But not to Him.

CHAPTER NINE

From Hair to Eternity

When the 1980s arrived, Americans were tired of being miserable. They had just lost a long war. They'd been through almost two decades of civil strife and domestic terrorism. Everyone was exhausted. The Age of Aquarius, for all its idealistic virtues, got old really quickly. Americans were ready for something else.

It was out with the hippies and in with the yuppies.

President Ronald Reagan had a famous campaign ad which captured the zeitgeist. White picket fences, green lawns, rose bushes, and large front porches; people getting married, raising flags, delivering papers, and driving tractors. It was morning in America again.

People wanted to do two things in the '80s: have fun and make money. A lot of both. At least one of those was captured in the music. You had the theatrics, energy, and hedonism of heavy metal with over-the-top hair, outrageous outfits, and bombastic stage shows. Then there was New Wave, which was essentially soft punk mated with quirky pop synth where the men often looked like women, women looked like they were from Mars, and everyone looked like they had just attended a Warhol party. Michael Jackson emerged as the "King of Pop"; Madonna got her start dominating New York City clubs; Bruce Springsteen went from East Coast sensation to a heartland rocker; Peter Gabriel had the touch and "Shocked the Monkey." This is about the time "Video Killed the Radio Star" and MTV ruled the airwaves.

This cable station based out of New York City debuted on August 1, 1981, with the words, "Ladies and gentlemen, rock and roll. . . ." One of MTV's original slogans was, "You'll never look at music the same way again." An understatement, to be sure.

Early music videos were low-budget promos or concert clips. These videos were fun but not very professionally produced. Then Duran Duran, Michael Jackson, Madonna, and the Police brought their artistic sensibilities (and their record companies' inflated six-figure budgets) to the genre and changed the art form by shooting in exotic locales and using professional dancers, costumes, makeup, and famous directors. Now fans not only memorized the lyrics but took note of the distinctive choreography and dance sequences.

It was the first time in my life I didn't feel a strong connection to popular music. Yes, this decade produced some good music by artists such as the Cars, the Police, Tom Petty and the Heartbreakers, and the Traveling Wilburys. I thought videos by A-ha, Peter Gabriel, Tom Petty, and Prince were inventive and raised the level of artistry in the genre. But as far as me following these artists or going to one of their concerts, I had way too many other priorities.

I was closing in on thirty, and I was changing both inwardly and outwardly. The long hair, beard, and hippie threads were long gone. I was clean-shaven, my hair was cropped short, and I was settling into early middle age. Cathe and I had our first child, Christopher, purchased our first home, and were no longer driving beater cars. Our congregation grew up right alongside us, and we considered them part of our family. But even though I was growing older, I still had a young mindset.

Some people follow sports. Me? I have always been a fan of pop culture. It interests me. Technology, too. I'm an early adopter. I do not like to stay in the same place. I like to learn new things. I want to stay ahead of the curve, not trail behind it. I am also interested in certain trends, styles, movies, and music. It also gives me a way to talk to young people that need Christ as well as younger members of our congregation. The Apostle Paul understood this well. The Roman road system was the internet of his day, connecting a good percentage of the first-century world. Paul and others would walk those roads and look for ways to build bridges to their culture. Paul wrote that he wanted to "find common ground with everyone, doing everything I can to save some" (1 Corinthians 9:22).

The classic example of this is when the apostle spoke at the Areopagus at Mars Hill. This was the central meeting place in Greece. At that time, Athens was one of the cultural and intelletual centers of the world. There, Paul quoted some of the secular philosophers of the day to connect with his audience. First, he showed the emptiness of the philosophers' ideas, then proclaimed that a relationship with Christ was the answer. This is what I am attempting to do with this book and others I have written, like *Steve McQueen: The Salvation of an American Icon*, *Johnny Cash: The Redemption of an American Icon*, and others.

The great thing about the 1980s is that it gave us a lot to work with—musical acts that were as fun to watch as they were to listen to. If the '60s and '70s were all about substance, or at least appeared to be, the '80s were all about style. As the Pet Shop Boys sang: "I've got the brains, you've got the looks, let's make lots of money."

This was an era before internet streaming and downloads. Albums sold in the millions and concert attendance was measured in the hundreds of thousands. Do you remember the last time a contemporary rock star consistently sold out a stadium or large arena? Perhaps Kanye West or Taylor Swift? Miley Cyrus, Jay-Z, and Beyoncé also breathe that rarified air, but most musicians pulling those kinds of crowds today are legacy acts like Elton John, U2, Bruce Springsteen, the Eagles, the Rolling Stones, or Paul McCartney. My point is they were making bank and living the high life. God was not a part of the equation. They found out there's not a whole lot of room for a Bible on a table filled with coke dust, ash trays, and sticky whiskey glasses.

Some of these stars were already discovering parties weren't meant to last when, in the mid-1980s, the federal government tried crashing them for good.

It was September 19, 1985. Tipper Gore, the wife of U.S. Senator Al Gore, had bought a Prince album—the groundbreaking *Purple Rain*—for her eleven-year-old daughter. As with most Prince albums, some of the lyrics were risqué. Tipper found them "vulgar and embarrassing."

She literally made a federal case out of it. Along with a few other politicians' wives, she formed the Parents Music Resource Center (PMRC). The group suggested that albums be rated for content in the same way as movies.

In September 1985, the U.S. Senate held a hearing on what could be considered objectionable rock. Three musicians—John Denver, Frank Zappa, and Twisted Sister front man Dee Snider—testified. (Now that would have been an interesting lineup for a concert, almost as strange as Jimi Hendrix opening for the Monkees, which did happen in 1967.)

Snider—all 6'1" of him—strode into the hearing chamber, wearing sunglasses, a sleeveless denim jacket, tight jeans, and a gold cross around his neck, his permed blonde hair flowing like a lion's mane. People had told him to wear a suit and to tie his hair back.

"No, I'm going to put on my uniform," he replied. "This is my uniform."[1]

He took off the jacket, pulled a folded sheaf of papers from his back pocket, and sat down. The gavel rapped, and Committee Chairman John Danforth said, "Mr. Snider, thank you for being here."

"I don't know whether it's morning or afternoon, so I'll say both: good morning and good afternoon," Snider replied in his heavy western Long Island accent. He went on to introduce himself as a husband and father.

"I was born and raised a Christian, and I still adhere to those principles. Believe it or not, I do not drink, I do not smoke, and I do not do drugs. I do play and write the songs for a band called Twisted Sister that is classified as heavy metal, and I pride myself on writing songs that are consistent with my above-mentioned beliefs."

Snider went on from there to calmly, coolly, and logically devastate the PMRC's criticisms of his music and his band:

> Where I am in complete agreement with the PMRC, as well as the national PTA and probably most of the parents on this committee, is that it is my job as a parent to monitor what my children see, hear, and read during their pre-teen years. The full responsibility falls on the

shoulders of my wife and me because there is no one else capable of making these judgments for us. Parents can thank the PMRC for reminding them there is no substitute for parental guidance, but that is where the PMRC's job ends.[2]

Who knew that a rock star could be so practical?

It was like watching an extremely hairy trial lawyer minted at Harvard Law School destroy his opposition with an opening statement. When senators tossed loaded questions at Snider, he swatted them away with the ease of a cat batting moths.

He wasn't going to take it anymore.

Despite the fact that nineteen record companies agreed to the PMRC's terms, the only lasting results of this fracas were that occasionally you'd have to buy a disc with a warning sticker (which usually helped sell more units), and that people found out Dee Snider was a smart, fairly conservative guy. Who knew? For him, being sober, having been raised in a Christian home, and also being a metal musician were not mutually exclusive identities.

• • •

W.A.S.P., a Los Angeles metal band, was another big target of the PMRC in the 1980s because of their expletive-laced songs and album titles. Some even thought the band name stood for "We Are Satan's People," but the media and hypervigilant parents tended to get a little carried away during the "Satanic panic" of the 1980s. (It's worth noting that the band's first vinyl release included the phrase "We Are Sexual Perverts" around the center label, and the band's raunchy titles and lyrics would certainly suggest that was a real possibility—but the band members themselves have only said that they thought the periods would make the band name stand out.[3]) In my opinion, they did it to stand out from the pack and ultimately sell more records.

The band emerged from the same Sunset Strip scene that produced Mötley Crüe, Quiet Riot, Ratt, and others. They wore outrageous makeup, teased their hair high, dressed in leather and chains, and sported long black gloves and knee-high platform boots. Their act was replete with lots of feathers, swords, and fake blood. They placed young women on torture racks and nuns on crosses. Their brand of shock rock sold more than twelve million copies and touted the joys of running wild in the streets, shooting from the hip, and "not needing no doctor."

Lead singer Blackie Lawless (real name Steven Edward Duren) was a lot like Dee Snider in that he was tall (6'4"), and he didn't drink, smoke, or take drugs. His rebellion came from within.

Lawless was raised in a religious household; his uncle was a preacher, his father was a Sunday School superintendent, and his grandfather was a deacon. But by the time he reached his teens, Lawless had had his fill and turned his back on the church.

"I started seeing things that weren't making sense," he later said. "I started looking at a lot of it as indoctrination, trying to get people to think *their* way instead of thinking for themselves. That really bothered me, so when I left the church I went as far away as you could go."[4]

He studied the occult for three years and even dated a witch who often chanted while sitting inside a pentagram. At the time, none of this fazed Lawless.

For two decades, Steven Edward Duren thought he was angry at God. Then one day, he realized he wasn't. Instead, he realized that he was angry at man for the indoctrination he saw taking place in the church.

"I had to go find out the truth for myself, so I faced it and started studying," he later said.

> Quite honestly, I was trying to disprove the Bible. And one day I'm reading, and I thought, *I'm reading the living word of the living God*, and that's when it hit me. I had to get out from underneath some bad doctrine to go find the truth for myself, and that was a long, long journey. I see it all the time—I watch people come from different denominations and their head is all screwed up and they've got weird ideas because they're listening to the ideas of men. You can see for the last two thousand years, there's different versions of that all over the place.[5]

Lawless said these days he lives by faith, and that means a personal relationship with Christ. He wrote of that relationship brilliantly in his 2015 song, "Jesus, I Need You Now."

* * *

Rudy Sarzo has always lived by faith. He didn't become a Christian out of a need to be moral or because he led a decadent lifestyle. The bassist for Ozzy Osbourne, and later Quiet Riot, was raised in the Catholic faith, and from a young age had his feet planted firmly on the ground. He faced many temptations as a rock star but consistently turned his back on the things he knew were destructive, even if it might cost him a lucrative gig. Such was the case when he auditioned for Osbourne, rock's "Prince of Darkness."

Sarzo had been eking it out on the LA rock scene for a few years, landing gigs with Quiet Riot and Angel, a glam rock band that dressed in white satin. Nothing was clicking. At his lowest point, he was sleeping on the floor of a friend's apartment, and yet his faith remained steadfast. Then he received a call from his friend, guitarist Randy Rhoads, saying that Osbourne wanted him to audition for his band.

But this was no audition; it was more like the last temptation of Christ.

When Sarzo met Ozzy and his wife Sharon (who ran his business affairs) at their home, they offered the usual rock star libations: vodka and cocaine. He politely declined each, thinking it could possibly be a test. Looking back, Sarzo said he couldn't blame the couple for making those offers; he later described them as two of the kindest, most caring people he had ever known.

"Ozzy and Sharon Osbourne had no idea who I was. They went on Randy Rhoads's recommendation," Sarzo said. "They wanted to know, what if I turn into a drug addict or an alcoholic in the middle of the tour? What if I turn into someone who's not responsible on stage? They had to find out themselves. They tested me because they wanted to know about my character."[6]

In time, the Osbournes would discover Sarzo's character was beyond reproach. He was not only a talented and reliable musician, but he was extremely focused and humble to boot. When Sarzo got the Ozzy gig, he promised God that he would glorify Him and not do anything to denigrate himself or his Lord—even in the most trying of times.

The most trying day came on March 19, 1982—a game-changer for everyone in the band and crew, and a day that changed Sarzo's life forever. After pulling an all-nighter in Knoxville, Tennessee, the band's golden-brown tour bus traveled 650 miles to Leesburg, Florida, and stayed there in preparation for a show in nearby Orlando. The band parked the bus approximately sixty feet from a Georgian-style mansion that bordered a private airstrip.

Their bus driver, Andy Aycock, a former commercial pilot, commandeered a small, single-engine 1955 Beechcraft Bonanza F35 to take Rhoads and Rachel Youngblood, the band's fifty-year-old seamstress, up in the air that morning. Rudy decided to sleep in.

Andy "buzzed" the tour bus three times at speeds of 140 to 180 mph. On the fourth pass, the left wing of the plane clipped the back of the bus, tearing a six-foot gash through the roof, and then spiraled out of control. It crossed over the bus and decapitated a large pine tree before crashing through the estate's garage. The Beechcraft exploded and burned on impact, incinerating the two cars in the garage and killing everyone on board. The bodies inside the plane were burned beyond recognition. Sarzo wanted to rush in to save his friend, but a fireman stopped him.

"Son, you don't want to go in there," he said. "Just remember them the way they looked the last time you saw them alive."[7]

As traumatic as it was, Randy Rhoads's death didn't shake Rudy Sarzo's steadfast faith or make him question why God would take the life of his friend at the age of twenty-five.

"I never questioned my faith during that whole time. I tried to figure things out, to make sense of things," Sarzo said. "I grieved and somehow learned to live with the passing of a friend—somebody who I owed my career to, someone who I believed saved our lives by turning the plane from crashing into the bus when we were sleeping and just clipping it instead."[8]

Decades after that horrible accident, Sarzo has kept good on his promise by continuing to put God and others first.

"People think of rock stars as guys who can have as many chicks as they want, can drink like fish, do a bunch of drugs, and be an ass on a daily basis," he said. "No, to me, that is a rock and roll casualty. A rock star is someone like Bruce Springsteen, Bono,

Sting—people who take their musical accomplishments and then turn around and help others."[9]

Who would have thought?

. . .

C. C. DeVille of Poison was in no place to help others for a few decades. The lead guitarist for one of the '80s' most popular charting hair bands ("Every Rose Has Its Thorn") was so wasted on drugs and alcohol most of the time that one critic said, "He wasn't high. He was in another dimension." If you watch Poison's eye-popping videos from that period, DeVille is the guitarist who looks like an insane street person with a mop of bleach-blonde hair, contorted facial expressions, and body spasms.

It wasn't an act, either. DeVille was so high most of the time he didn't know where he was. Sometimes he didn't know what he was supposed to be playing. A legendary example of that is the 1991 MTV Video Music Awards. Sporting a pink dye job that made him look like a demented troll doll, DeVille launched into the wrong song when Poison took the stage. Emcee Arsenio Hall nervously tried to paper over the disaster in front of the live audience, but DeVille was relentless, capering around the stage, leering with a jack-o-lantern smile, and not so much playing his guitar as playing with it. Lead singer Bret Michaels gamely tried to play along like the pacifying mother at a Thanksgiving dinner gone horribly wrong, but it was hopeless. A crew member finally had to unplug DeVille's amplifier, but it was too late. The damage had already been done.

The fiasco has since gone down as one of the top ten classic drugged-out rock performances. Backstage, Michaels and DeVille got into the worst of their many fistfights. They might have looked like dressed-up glam girls, but they brawled like Marines. It was the end of Poison for DeVille. He was kicked out of the band and quickly replaced with another guitarist.

But that episode didn't sober him up. He had a lot of "lost years" after that—fifteen of them, to be precise.

The end of the party came one night in August 2005. While driving black-out drunk, he hit four parked cars while backing out of his girlfriend's driveway in Los Angeles. Police found him crawling along the roadside two blocks away. He pled no contest to driving while intoxicated and was sentenced to jail for eighty days. He was also put on five years' probation, fined $1,000, and forced to surrender his driver's license for a year. The time in jail gave DeVille's forty-three-year-old body a chance to recuperate after decades of partying and substance abuse.

"I would do drugs and have sex. I would do drugs and write a song. I would do drugs and socialize with people. Everything was based around the drugs," DeVille said of his life. "Once I stopped doing the drugs, I had to relearn all my people skills. I had to relearn how to live."[10]

DeVille thinks the accident was the wake-up call he so desperately needed and that, in the end, he's a very fortunate man.

"I was lucky that I got in enough trouble to wake myself up, but not enough trouble that I had to live with the fact that I killed someone for the rest of my life," he said. "I'm just lucky enough to not have that rage that drugs do to you. You get this rage and this chip on your shoulder, and you tend to alienate everyone who loves you. It's awful. I'm really glad I'm where I'm at now."[11]

Waking up from drugs also meant waking up to God. DeVille realized that he was blessed with God's grace and was later mentored by a pastor in Nashville.

In an interview, he said, "I called on the Lord. The cars didn't do it. The houses didn't do it. Making others feel less than me didn't do it. Me trying to inflate my own self didn't do it. The Lord's grace in not bullying me and looking at His grace is what makes me change. I don't know anything that works like that.

"If I have a boss and he yells at me and bullies me, he's in a state of authority and I'm in a state of someone who's listening. Yet, I don't feel like I wanna be like him. The Lord, through love, through patience, through His grace . . . you wanna get closer."[12]

Having a son helped DeVille understand unconditional love—the kind of love that God has shown to him over the years, including throughout his drug-and-alcohol-hazed journey. And now he's giving it back to others in a loving and kind way.

"Sometimes people want to hear it from someone who is flawed, and I'm more than happy to take what has happened to me negatively and try to put a positive spin on it now," DeVille said. "Going through those mistakes is bad, but if there's a lesson, and if I can talk about these mistakes, now it becomes good. I feel blessed. Today, I feel great."[13]

* * *

Megadeth and Metallica. Heavy metal doesn't get any harder than that. Dave Mustaine, who was in both bands, has the constitution of Keith Richards but doesn't get the credit for it. He traveled two dark roads: Baptized as a Lutheran and brought up as a Jehovah's Witness, he ended up getting into witchcraft, black magic, and Satanism. In the other lane was chemical abuse. It started with alcohol and pot, swiftly followed by cocaine and heroin. In Metallica's early days, Mustaine recalled, "If we had enough money to get our heroin and a hot dog, it was a good day."[14]

As the band's lead guitarist, Mustaine was considered a major talent with a major problem and major attitude. He played like an angel, but he drank like a demon.

"I would drink and have fun until someone would refute something I had said," Mustaine said. "And then it was war, baby."[15]

One of his highs was violence. He was an "Are you looking at me?" kind of drunk. Fights started at the drop of a hat. He woke up with injuries on top of his hangovers, quarreled with other bands, and sometimes would punch out his own bandmates, which ultimately got him kicked out of Metallica. When they gave him the pink slip in late 1983, they didn't give him a plane ticket: it was a bus ticket from the Port Authority in New York City—a place not many rock stars see at the height of their fame—back to LA.

Mustaine recovered quickly professionally. He formed another band: Megadeth, considered one of the four pillars of the heavy/thrash metal sound. As the band rose in popularity, so did Mustaine's substance abuse. He and the bandmates hired their drug dealer to be their manager based on what he could provide for them; their most important business decision was getting high. Nothing was normal, including their sleep patterns.

"I never went to sleep," Mustaine said. "I passed out."[16]

Toward the end of 2001, Mustaine showed up to a video shoot for VH1's popular *Behind the Music* series. He was so fried on a cocktail of drugs, including heroin, that he couldn't sing and play guitar at the same time. His singing and playing ultimately had to be recorded separately for that show. In March 1989, he was arrested for impaired driving—"impaired" being the key word here.

"When I got arrested, I had nine different chemicals in my body," he said.[17]

He was forced to enter rehab. It didn't take at first. Mustaine ended up going back fifteen times. While obviously most of it didn't work, the spiritual component of Alcoholics Anonymous resonated. In a moment of serenity, he says he found God.

More than that: in 2002, Mustaine was born again.

"Frankly, for me, I don't believe in religion," he said. "I have a personal relationship with Christ, and that's it. I don't push that on anybody; it's private. I kind of leave it there."[18]

Talk about His power. Who else but God Almighty could transform a hedonistic '80s heavy metal star into a devout Christian? All of these men had the fame, the wealth, the influence, the cars, the houses, and the jets, but in the end, they were powerless against themselves. Managers, producers, mothers, fathers, wives, girlfriends—no one could tell them what to do.

But in the end, they all found a new beginning.

Here is a takeaway truth: God goes out of his way to reach unexpected people in unexpected ways in unexpected places. No one is beyond the reach of God. No one.

Today, most of these rockers no longer can squeeze into spandex, keep their hair long or teased high, wear mascara, or body surf on waves of Wild Turkey. Instead of flashing their heavy metal horns, they kneel and pray.

From hair to eternity.

CHAPTER TEN

Tell Me All Your Thoughts on God

The 1990s were great because they were a lot like the 1950s: not a lot happened.

The decade has been called "the holiday from history." Communism had fallen hard and there were no major wars. A young and hip presidential candidate named Bill Clinton played saxophone on *The Arsenio Hall Show* while the economy roared at 4 percent per year. The baby boomers had cut their hair and were running just about everything. Some in the generation behind them—Generation X—didn't seem to care about anything other than having a good time and making money.

There was some unrest. Terrorists blew up a truck bomb underneath the World Trade Center, but everyone looked at that as a one-off. Domestic terrorists took their share of attention (like blowing up a federal building in Oklahoma City), but mostly they hid out in places like Ruby Ridge or Waco, where federal agents hitched up the cavalry to hunt them down.

The 1990s were a free-for-all for music, but not necessarily a reflection of the culture. A reaction to the highly stylized metal bands and glam rock emerged in the form of grunge and alternative, as did hip-hop, reggae, contemporary R&B, pop punk, industrial, boy bands, and a glitzier version of country where stars flew over audiences on wires and looked like movie stars. The *New York Times* called the '90s music scene "everything for everybody."

The numbers of CDs shipped annually almost quintupled, from 207 million to 937 million. *Billboard* charts were also altered to reflect actual sales as counted by SoundScan, a new tracking system that recorded sales of music products, such as albums and videos. The Top 40 splintered, and mainstream artists became scarce.

This was typified by Korn, an alternative rock-metal-industrial-rap-hip-hop group from Bakersfield, California. Korn had a niche following of skate rats with full-sleeve tattoos, shaved heads, and multiple piercings, but they sold more than forty million albums—an astounding number. They also racked up an impressive eight top-five albums, forty-one singles, and two Grammy awards.

Guitarist Brian Welch grew up in difficult home. His father was a good man, by and large. But when he drank, he was "scary," according to Welch. Brian was bullied at school, where fellow students gave him the nickname "Head" because they said his head was too big for his body.

"It seems funny now, but at the time it really made me sad," Welch said. "I walked around feeling like I looked like a big-headed freak."[1]

Children of alcoholics often have a common trait: they are escape artists. Welch's escapes were shoplifting, slasher films, and heavy metal music. He also adopted the heavy metal look and lifestyle. After an experimentation with pot left him terrified, he began hanging around an old friend named Kevin who lived down the street.

Kevin's family were happy Christians. Sunday church, family dinners, and convivial gatherings were the norm. Brian loved it all. One day, Kevin's mother suggested that he, too, could experience the peace of Jesus Christ if he'd ask Him to come into his heart. Later that night in the basement of his home, the thirteen-year-old Head did so. As he recalled, "I felt something."[2]

But it didn't last. High school started, he and Kevin drifted apart, and Brian made new friends. They ended up being the centerpiece of Korn: Jonathan Davis, James "Munky" Shaffer, Reginald "Fieldy" Arvizu, and David Silveria. In a short time, they drifted over to Huntington Beach and officially formed Korn in the summer of 1993. A year later, they went from working at Pizza Hut to being a household name. Their debut album sold two million copies and gave birth to four singles. It also spawned an addiction to meth and other bad lifestyle choices. Welch was swallowed by it all.

"I was tripping out. We were all tripping out," he later said. "We're on MTV every day. We've got private jets, security guards, doing in-store appearances with five thousand people showing up. Girls are crying when they look at me—I mean, I was driving a beat-up Toyota Celica barely two years before, and now they were crying about being around me. Who am I?"[3]

A mess, some would say. After years of touring and recording, Welch struggled with addiction (meth, Xanax, sleeping pills, and alcohol), depression, and suicidal thoughts. He left the band in 2005 right before Korn was offered a new $23 million record deal. With the encouragement of a business partner and a church pastor, Welch began a slow journey back to the saving grace of Jesus Christ.

His conversion happened one evening when he was sitting at his computer and flipping through his Bible.

"I felt this presence around me, and it's like eternity opened up and Heaven touched me," Welch said. "I was frozen. I looked up and said, 'Father.' The only way to describe it is that I felt that I was home for the first time."[4]

Welch wasted no time getting baptized. He went to Israel, where an MTV camera crew filmed him getting dunked in the Jordan River where Jesus was immersed by John the Baptist. When Welch came up out of the water, he was crying tears of joy. He was reunited with the Savior.

In 2013, Welch reunited with Korn. He explained his decision this way:

> Everyone is broken in this world. There's so much divorce, hate, and unforgiveness. For people to see this, I think it's really uplifting. I never thought this would happen, and I'm not sure they did, either. The fans love it because a lot of them were like, suicidal, from broken homes and abuse. They looked up to us like their family, and to see their family split up was hard on them.

The reunification started a change within the band.

Reginald "Fieldy" Arvizu took millions of fans by surprise by becoming the second Korn member to become a Christian after Brian's conversion. As it turns out, his salvation experience had nothing to do with Welch's. He had plenty of his own problems.

Like Welch, Arvizu was a world-class partier with world-class addictions. Of course, he got started at a young age—five or six, by his estimation. He often fetched his dad's beers for him, which were kept in the fully stocked garage refrigerator. Eventually, he'd sneak out a few for himself and stash them in his bedroom, which was decorated with Budweiser pillows.

"My parents would tuck me into bed, and my mom'd be like, 'I love you,' and my dad would be like, 'Dream about Budweisers,'" Arvizu recalled. "I was destined to be a partier, I guess."[5]

Arvizu's parents got divorced when he was fourteen, and he was heartbroken. He stayed with his dad, a musician who said, "Us men . . . we've got to stick together."

"I was like, 'This is not going to hurt me,'" Arvizu said. "That's what I told my dad. 'I'm moving in with you. Let's get a keg, and let's throw a party and make music,' and I put a wall up to not feel the emotions. That's when it became full-on drinking and a way that nobody's going to hurt me. From that moment on, I never had a sober day."[6]

After becoming a bona fide rock star, Fieldy felt the rules no longer applied to him. In fact, he created his own set of rules to follow, which were basically no rules at all.

Arvizu said his excessive compulsions "turned me into a selfish, mean, and out-of-control jerk."[7] Outwardly, the bassist acted like he had it all under control. Internally, he knew there was a problem.

"I had my nights of being in hotel rooms and destroying them by myself, crying because I'd wake up in the morning feeling so bad from partying," he said. "I'd be shaking. I'd wake up and throw up in the morning. I'm like, 'Man, I can't handle this.' So I would just take some Xanax or Ativan and let that kick in and I'd just be wasted again. It'd bring you so down, then [I would] smoke weed after that. Then night would come, and I could start drinking."[8]

Arvizu did finally sober up when his father was diagnosed with cancer. His father had become a Christian, and in a moment of serenity, expressed one dying wish: that his son finally let go of his anger and get right with God.

Fieldy initially said a prayer out of desperation in 2005, but nothing happened. He tried it again a few days later at the prompting of his wife, Dena, but with great warmth and sincerity. This time it changed his life.

"I had chills throughout my whole body, almost like a coldness," he later said.

> I was crying. I tell a lot of people that you can do the prayer with your brain, but that's not going to do anything. You must do it with your heart. When I accepted Christ, now I'm like, "Okay, I'm going to pray for some of these things that I'm a slave to." It went in steps. So that I was set free with no withdrawals. No craving. I stopped everything down to weed and the pills. I just stopped.[9]

Twenty years of filling his body with toxins stopped in an instant. After he got sober, Arvizu spent a year apologizing to all the people he had wronged. Almost all the wreckage had been wreaked under the influence of chemicals. He constantly prayed and asked for forgiveness, especially from his bandmates, close friends, and his wife. Some apologies went better than others. He was on a new journey—one that made many people happy and more than a few uncomfortable.

Arvizu began reading God's Word every day, studying it, dissecting it, applying it to his life. The New Testament became his life's guide.

"By the time I finished the New Testament, everything became crystal clear," he said. "Life was no longer complicated. It was simple because every single answer to life's dilemmas was in those pages."[10]

Another life changed. Fieldy could have been another rock tragedy, but thankfully his story took a turn toward Christ. Fieldy and Brian have both attended our church, Harvest Orange County. I was at a Sturgis event several years ago and rode my Harley in the pitch dark for miles to an event where Korn was performing. They put on quite a show and still have a big legion of fans. I thank God for how He intervened in the life of Fieldy and Head. They live in a world where a little light goes a long way. They are both still works in progress. Aren't we all?

. . .

Percussionist Sheila E. had no drug or alcohol issues to contend with. "The Glamorous Life" singer and Prince protégé who made such a splash in the 1980s was physically and emotionally exhausted by the early 1990s, after decades of endless tours where she beat on drums for hours at a time—wearing six-inch stiletto heels, no less.

Sheila Escovedo was bit by the entertainment bug at age five. Her father, Pete, was the leader of Azteca, a popular Bay Area Latin-jazz fusion band. One night he invited his little girl on stage at Sweet's Ballroom in Oakland to play a solo on the congas in front of three thousand people. The crowd went nuts, and Sheila spent the rest of her childhood and teen years preparing for her vocation as a musician. She was recruited into her father's band while in high school, appearing on two of his albums.

She was raised Catholic but admits she only went to church because her parents forced her to go. When she turned eighteen, she gave her heart to the Lord. But after doing some session work for some very famous Christians, she was quickly disenchanted.

"I saw how they acted, and I said, 'I don't want to be a Christian because the things that they are doing are so wrong,'" she said. "I felt I was better off not being a Christian. I was very discouraged because of how Christians were acting and because, back then 'the thing' was to be or become born again. It was like a fad, you know? So, I just got turned off."[11]

Soon after that, she met Prince. Their musical association quickly thrust her into the public spotlight, and her career hit the stratosphere.

But after years of touring, studio sessions, and punishing drumbeats, every part of her body ached—ankles, calves, hands, wrists, arms, elbows, shoulders, and neck. Deep-tissue massages usually reinvigorated her, but as she entered her mid-thirties, she graduated to a course of rigorous acupuncture. Many treatments required more than fifty needles in her body at a time.

The Chinese have embraced and used this treatment for centuries, believing the needles help the blood and the energy flow—but after one session, Sheila E. found it hard to breathe. One day she sneezed, her back gave out, and she fell to the ground. Her body spasmed and seized, and she was paralyzed for almost two weeks.

Desperate to find an answer for why she was immobile, she flew a doctor from Los Angeles to Minneapolis. He carried out a series of tests; an X-ray revealed her body had become twisted from the wear and tear of playing drums. He also discovered that her left lung was 80 percent collapsed from an acupuncturist's needle, which was what had left her struggling to breathe. Compounding the problem were all the medications she had to take, which left her sick and with no appetite. Her weight dropped from 120 to 85 pounds.

"My cousin Ia came to live with me and spoon-fed me like a baby," Sheila recalled. "Because I had so little energy, it sometimes took me fifteen minutes to down a spoonful of mashed potatoes. I thought I was going to die in that house."[12]

She lay in her bed crying and praying to God for another chance at life. She even asked a friend in Israel to send her holy water, thinking that might heal her. When she could muster the strength, she read her Bible, looking for a possible cure in the Scriptures. She even slept with the Bible on her chest, thinking its proximity might help.

Eventually, her body recovered because of all the deep rest. However, she was now afraid to venture outside. Her home was her comfort zone, and she didn't want to leave. She had been indoors for a good month. Finally, her cousin forced her to go outside, thinking the fresh air would reinvigorate her mind and spirit. It did.

"As soon as I stepped out into the sunny brightness of the day, I dropped to my knees in gratitude and kissed a crack in the pavement," Sheila said. "Even that pavement was beautiful."[13]

She noticed the beautiful color of God's landscape—the green grass, the white clouds, and blue sky. She walked over to a tree to give it a mighty hug, then lay back in the grass and investigated the sky.

"God had given all of this to me," she said. "And it took nearly losing myself to truly see it. I had taken so much for granted. I thought I needed money and belongings and applause, but all I needed was this."[14]

But she needed Christ, too. Sheila began attending church and reading the Scriptures regularly. She made a personal commitment to Jesus Christ and demonstrated it by doing ministry work, making sure to be a blessing to someone or something every day of the week.

"For me, religion is more than following rules and laws," she said. "The divine connection is having faith, honoring the Word, and having a spiritual relationship with God."[15]

. . .

Sheila E. remains a beloved figure—but Creed has been called "the most hated band in history."

The criticisms: "They try too hard." "A cheap version of Pearl Jam." "Music that sounds like grunge in the same way a pot of coffee might taste if you used the same grounds six times in a row." "Radio hits that people liked until they had heard them 1,000 times too many."

Then there was lead singer Scott Stapp. He was called a "fame hound." Critics felt that his posturing on stage and in videos was too much to take. One joke that made the rounds on the internet: "How do you drown the lead singer of Creed? Tie a mirror to the bottom of the ocean."

Stapp did a good job of drowning himself—getting kicked off planes for being too drunk, brawling in barrooms, notoriously arriving at one concert where he was too wasted to sing (or stand up), and getting arrested for domestic violence after he threw an orange juice bottle at his wife's head. And the coup de grace: a psychotic episode brought on by drugs and alcohol during which he drifted around the country, following an angel he saw on the hood of his car.

Stapp was raised as a Christian, although more out of fear than love. His stepfather was a strict Pentecostal who literally tried to beat the Gospel into him. Stapp was forced to copy long passages from the Bible by hand as punishment for wrongdoing. His step-father once punished him for coming home with a 3.5 GPA because it wasn't a 4.0.

"A Christian home according to God's Word is much different than what I was raised in," he said years later. "Yes, there was talk of Christ and there was church three times a week, but there was discipline and abuse in the name of God. It wasn't how a Christian home should be."[16]

He ran away at seventeen, unable to endure it anymore.

In 1994, Stapp formed Creed with a high school friend. Their first album was released three years later and sold six million copies. Four singles reached the Top Three on *Billboard's* Hot Mainstream Rock Tracks chart. The album was followed in 1999 by *Human Clay*, which was an immediate success—certified diamond, and eleven times platinum.

Fame came quickly, which Stapp said amplified all his problems. He became addicted to Percocet, Xanax, and prednisone, among other substances. What he did not become addicted to was being part of the band. He wasn't focused on the music or the tours; a clothing line and movie offers distracted him.

"He definitely had his plate full, whether it was professional or personal," drummer Scott Phillips said. "He always had the cell phone going."[17]

The final straw for the band, fans, and critics came on December 29, 2002, in Chicago. Plenty of people go to concerts and complain about them, but that Creed show was so bad fans filed a class action lawsuit. It may hold a place in rock history as the first time music lovers took legal action against a band for being lousy.

According to Cook County Circuit Court filings, Stapp was so "intoxicated and/or medicated that he was unable to sing the lyrics of a single Creed song." Instead, he "left the stage on several occasions during songs for long periods of time, rolled around on the floor of the stage in apparent pain or distress and [finally] appeared to pass out."

The case was eventually dismissed; the judge said deciding what constituted a good show and a bad one was "no business of the judiciary."

In 2004, after nearly ten years together and more than twenty-four million albums sold, Creed broke up.

And so did Stapp. In 2005, he got in a brawl with members of the band 311 at the Harbor Court Hotel in Baltimore. Stapp was doing shots, being loud and obnoxious, and made "a disrespectful comment to my wife that I'd rather not repeat," said 311's front man, SA Martinez.[18]

He gave another noteworthy performance as "the drunk everyone hates" on a taping of *Casino Cinema*, a Spike TV programming block hosted by *Sopranos* star Steve Schirripa and Beth Ostrosky, Howard Stern's wife. The show, which was played around the commercial breaks of a film, featured the hosts teaching the audience how to play a casino game.

The game that night, ironically, was poker. Stapp embodied every bad experience with someone who's drunk, every negative behavior amped up to ten: braggadocious, violent, inappropriate, insulting, oblivious. He swore incessantly, hit on Ostrosky, was rude to Schirripa (who handled everything with aplomb and grace), slurred his speech, and generally made a fool of himself. "I make more money than Howard," he told Ostrosky at one point.

That incident landed him in rehab and, as is so frequent, he was sober for the thirty-one days he lived there. But the outside world held brighter and more alluring lights.

A year later, in February 2006, mere hours after getting married, Stapp was busted for public intoxication in Los Angeles as the couple were en route to their honeymoon in Hawaii. Later that year in Miami, he jumped over a balcony and fell forty feet, fracturing his skull and breaking his hip and nose. He said it was a suicide attempt.

Then the crazy really came! In November 2014, Stapp filmed a video claiming he was living in his car and a Holiday Inn and was going without food for days at a time. He also asked viewers to donate $480,000 so he could write a book and record a solo album.

By spring the following year, he had begun believing he was part of the CIA and assigned the task of assassinating President Obama. When his wife, Jaclyn, filed for divorce, she claimed he had been on amphetamines, crystal meth, and steroids for weeks at a time.

For the next three long months, friends and family watched Stapp unravel. He later claimed he had a psychotic break that was induced by alcohol and drug abuse.

He began an intensive program in a facility that treats both addiction and mental health issues. He received a conclusive diagnosis: bipolar disorder, a condition that causes unexpected shifts in mood, energy, and activity levels.

"It made sense," said Jaclyn. "I definitely knew there was something going on for years, but I couldn't pinpoint what it was."[19]

Stapp took medication for his disorder, worked through a twelve-step program, and met with a sponsor. A repurposing started to happen.

"I was in a valley. As I finally confessed, that's when God repurposed and started the process of removing the shame, guilt, and anger—at least cutting away the big trees of it and planting in me a desire to help," he later said. "Maybe because of the platform He gave me, maybe there are others out there who have gone through similar situations who can hear my story and take something from it."[20]

• • •

In the 1990s, you couldn't touch MC Hammer (born Stanley Burrell). The first rapper to enjoy mainstream success, he went from selling his albums out of the trunk of his car to becoming a superstar who sold more than twenty-five million albums worldwide. He also won three Grammys, seven American Music Awards, and two MTV Awards.

Hammer's act was characterized by his high-energy dancing—his talent has been compared to Michael Jackson's—his baggy parachute pants, and a huge team of backup dancers. His stage name was a take on "emcee"—short for "Master of Ceremonies." And he was born to play that role.

Burrell's father was a professional poker player, and his mother was a secretary. Stanley lived with them and his eight siblings in a three-bedroom apartment in Oakland, California, when he was young. He grew up Pentecostal and acknowledges that he strayed from his faith during his success.

Hammer's fall didn't come through drugs or alcohol. Instead, he was simply a tragic business failure. He underwrote a huge entourage that followed him practically everywhere, but his dwindling album sales, unpaid loans, large payroll, and lavish lifestyle led him to declare bankruptcy in 1996.

Hammer made an initial commitment to Christ in 1984. He attended Bible studies and church meetings almost daily. He was also active on an outreach team with a street ministry. Simultaneously, a gospel group he formed, the Holy Ghost Boys, produced a single called "Son of the King," which eventually became one of Hammer's biggest hits.

But a change came in 1988. A Capitol Records exec caught his act in an Oakland Club and signed him to a contract with a $1.7

million advance. Capitol re-released his first album, *Feel the Power*, as *Let's Get It Started*. It produced three Top Ten singles and sold over a million copies.

Thankful for the success, Hammer promised God he would include one song of praise on each album. He kept his word, but fortune gradually sucked him into what he calls "some serious junk." He began to slide into sin.

He was making $33 million per year but spent it almost as soon as he earned it. He bought a $9 million mansion on twelve acres in California—where land is anything but inexpensive. There were two swimming pools with computer-controlled thermostats, a reflecting pool, a nine-car garage and, inside the house, three master bedrooms, four dishwashers, a media room, an exercise room, a recording studio, and a rehearsal hall. At his peak, Hammer owned seventeen cars and a Boeing 727.

But by 1996, he was $13 million in debt. "My priorities were out of order," he told *Ebony*. "My priorities should have always been God, family, community, and then business. Instead, they had been business, business, and business."[21] He moved his wife, Stephanie, and four children to a rental home in Tracy, California, shortly after he filed for bankruptcy that April.

The following year, Hammer rediscovered his faith. He was ordained in the Church of God in Christ and set his life on a new course.

"Previously, being a prodigal son took me away from the relationship that I once knew. There came a point where I wanted to just get back home. Get back to the place . . . I once had in my relationship with Jesus," he said.

"Whether the bankruptcy played any role in my refocusing, that's great. Hallelujah, I hope it did! But the most important part of what occurred to me was love, missing the love of God in the way that I had known it."[22]

Like everything else in his life, he announced the rekindling of his love for God in classic Hammer style. At the World Gospel '97 extravaganza in Barbados, through billows of smoke and with fireworks exploding above his head, Hammer, wearing a metallic gold space suit, rose from beneath a stage to sing about his renewed faith in God.

Hammer now devotes his time to prison and youth ministries. He is still MC Hammer, but now the MC stands for "Man of Christ." I met him at a taping for a TV show some years ago and was impressed by his devotion and demeanor. I thank God that the Lord got hold of him and redirected his life.

Today, all these stars are symbols of resilience and what can happen when God is at the top of their personal charts. The Lord can reach unexpected people in unexpected places.

Brian "Head" Welch, Reginald "Fieldy" Arvizu, Sheila E., Scott Stapp, and MC Hammer—they all hit bottom before they looked up.

It basically comes down to this: when you get to the end of yourself, you get to the beginning of God.

CHAPTER ELEVEN

Jesus, Take the Wheel

Instead of partying like it was 1999, the 2000s kicked off with fear. The Y2K scare had everyone believing that planes would fall out of the sky, ATMs wouldn't work, and the power grid would go dark. None of that happened, but real terror was right around the corner, as someone in the Middle East was plotting to fly planes into skyscrapers.

Going to the airport and taking trips changed forever. What was once fun became an ordeal. A color-coded terror alert was on the news every night, and it still hasn't returned to the lowest level.

Scares kept coming, one after another. With the threat of anthrax, people were scared of getting the mail. Mass shootings made people leery of going to the mall, church, concerts, restaurants, and other public places. As reality became harsher, people increasingly sought to escape from it through the internet and reality TV (which was anything but real).

But things were about to get a lot worse.

In 2008, the Great Recession hit almost everyone. People lost jobs, savings, and homes. Banks that had been in business for more than a century practically vanished overnight. Millions of new houses stood vacant or half-finished across the country.

Things looked as bleak as they had in the late 1960s, but this time there was no Bob Dylan, John Lennon, or Crosby, Stills & Nash to help make sense of it or to ease our pain. Technology overtook music's prominence in pop culture. Everything became secondary to technology. For the first time since the invention of the automobile, kids wanted a new phone, not a new car. Millennials no longer wanted any physical products. If they wanted to read a book, they simply downloaded it to their iPad or iPhone. If they wanted a new album, same thing. The experience of browsing through the local record store had gone the way of going to the local butcher.

Steve Jobs was the new John Lennon.

Kids no longer heard the siren call of music; now, music was simply a byproduct of technology. Instead of being the first to own a new album, the cool thing was to be the first to own a new app or ringtone. Music still mattered, but it had changed and splintered. There were no longer any universally loved rock gods; instead, there was a star for every niche.

Rock music, the dominant language of youth since the 1950s, had now fallen into the realm of oddities like collecting books and vinyl albums. It still existed, but it held little allure. Real bands that wrote their own songs and played their own instruments no longer existed—or if they did, they broke up after their second or third album when they discovered going solo meant they wouldn't have to divvy up the paycheck. Some with more entrepreneurial spirits discovered, like Sammy Hagar and Dr. Dre, that there's more money in creating a line of tequila or starting a new line of headphones. Rock stars were no longer pigeonholed into just creating music; they were now entertainment brands, which meant they were as much about tequila, hoodies, and sneakers as they were about singles. Nobody exemplifies that more than Kanye West, who is estimated to be worth about $1.8 billion through his endorsement deals with The Gap and Adidas, not to mention his own fashion line and wellness and beauty products. He's now looking to move into the tech realm.

In many ways, Justin Bieber's popularity rivaled Kanye's, but with a different demographic: young girls. Bieber's popularity commenced when he was just thirteen. The ride was all fun and games at first—and then, like many famous people, he found himself at the end of Lonely Street.

The Canadian teen was discovered when American talent agent and record executive Scooter Braun came across some of Bieber's YouTube videos by accident. Braun arranged a deal with RBMB Records, which made the label very happy and prosperous. Bieber became the first artist to have seven songs from a debut record chart on the *Billboard* Hot 100 with his EP *My World*.[1] He was an instant international pop star, and it didn't take long for him to get lost in the wilderness of the world.

"I came from a small town in Stratford, Ontario, Canada," Bieber said. "I didn't have material things and was never motivated by money or fame. I just loved music. But as I became a teenager, I let my insecurities and frustrations dictate what I put my value in."[2]

The young superstar said millions of fans stroked his ego daily, telling him how much they loved him. While it was nice to hear, it was also damaging.

"You hear these things enough as a young boy and you actually start believing it," Bieber said. "So, by this point I was eighteen with no skills in the real world, with millions of dollars and access to whatever I wanted. This is a very scary concept for anyone."[3]

The charmed life got old very fast. Bieber said he allowed his ego and power to take over all his relationships, and each began to suffer as a result. There was also plenty of drinking, drugs, and promiscuity.

Marijuana was his gateway drug, which Bieber began to depend on heavily because of what he called his "crippling anxiety." He also turned to other highs for self-medication: alcohol, lean (a mixture of cough syrup, soda, and hard candy), MDMA, and psychedelic mushrooms. It got downright dangerous.

"My security and staff would come into my room at night to check my pulse," he said. "People don't know how serious it got. It was legit crazy scary. I was waking up in the morning and the first thing I was doing was popping pills and smoking a blunt and starting my day. It just got scary."[4]

Those afflictions, in tandem with a combination of Lyme disease and a chronic case of mononucleosis—plus a few brushes with the law—put Bieber in a very dark place.

"There was a sense of still yearning for more," he said. "It was like I had all this success, and it was still like: I'm still sad, and I'm still in pain. And I still have these unresolved issues. And I thought all the success was going to make everything good. And so for me, the drugs were a numbing agent to just continue to get through."[5]

Bieber said he felt no joy in anything he did. He later discovered through doctors that after years of being onstage, his dopamine levels had been maxed out and nothing got him excited anymore. He pushed friends and family members away, questioned the motives of everyone around him, and became joyless for a period.

Bieber was raised as a Christian by his mother, Pattie Mallette, but said he often struggled with forgiveness and shame.

However, hitting rock bottom finally made him question who this "Jesus guy was."

"I came to a place where I just was like, 'God, if You're real, I need You to help me, because I can't do this on my own,'" Bieber recalled. "Like, I'm struggling so hard. Every decision I make is out of my own selfish ego. So, I'm just like, 'What is it that You want from me? You put all these desires in my heart for me to sing and perform and to make music—where are these coming from? Why is this in my heart? What do You want me to do with it? What's the point? What is the point of everything? What is the point of me being on this planet?'"6

God didn't waste any time revealing a plan for Bieber's life. Now, only God and Justin Bieber know what that plan is—but by all appearances, he is on a much better track.

"The way I look at God and my relationship with Jesus is I'm not trying to earn God's love by doing good things," Bieber said. "God has already loved me for who I am before I did anything to earn or deserve it. It's a free gift by accepting Jesus, giving your life to Him, and what He did is the gift. The forgiveness is the thing that we look at and we go, 'You know, I'm going to worship You, God, because You gave me something so good.'"7

Bieber put his faith on full display in April 2021. That's when he released his surprise Easter EP *Freedom*, which raced to the top of the charts. The EP, which included a 3:16 timestamp on the cover, "is the first instance of the artist situating an entire project in an unapologetically Christian framework," according to the Religion News Service.8

• • •

Some musical artists have the good fortune of skipping the sex, drugs, and wretched excess that is a byproduct of their industry, and their lives and careers are clean from the start. Country star Carrie Underwood is a prime example of this.

Underwood, who rose to fame in 2005 after winning Season Four of *American Idol*, has remained steadfast in her faith, whether it be in person, on stage, or in song. The native Oklahoman was raised Baptist in a conservative Christian home in the small town of Checotah, a community of 3,400, "playing on dirt roads, climbing trees, and, of course, singing."

Sundays were reserved for church, and it wasn't something she avoided like most kids her age.

"Every Sunday, that was my stage," she said. "I loved opening the hymnals, and I'd try to sing real loud because I liked to!"[9]

"Just As I Am," the song that Billy Graham played at every one of his Crusades, was also played at the end of each church service.

"That was our altar call song. It was always the song that ended church," Underwood said. "I walked down the aisle to the front during the altar call to declare myself a follower of Christ."

Underwood continued singing in youth groups and in school productions, but with no formal vocal training. Through her teen years, she performed whenever she could: at parties, large gatherings, and county fairs with a country band. Besides singing, she excelled at playing guitar.

The twenty-one-year-old journalism major was in her last year of college at Northeastern State University in Tahlequah, Oklahoma, when she heard about the event that would end up changing her life.

While at home one weekend, she saw on the news that many people were in Cleveland, Ohio, sleeping outside in hopes of auditioning for the 2005 *American Idol* season. A couple of people told her she should try out. Underwood's mother offered to drive her to audition in St. Louis, Missouri, and the rest is history.

Underwood's victory on the show wasn't nearly as impressive as what she has done in the ensuing two decades. She is one of those rare superstars who happily shares her fame, fortune, and faith with everyone.

She's been a big advocate for causes that are near and dear to her heart: she supports a variety of animal-rights programs and organizations that benefit children and has set up a foundation in her hometown to help people in need. She has contributed to a fund for musical instruments and various school supplies, including Chromebooks, in her former Oklahoma high school district. Underwood has also donated large sums to Save the Children, made visits to St. Jude's Children's Research Hospital, and does public service announcements for several worthy organizations.

"Everybody has the power to do something, to be a contributing force," Underwood said, "and I would rather people look back on my life and say, 'She made the world a better place.' We can all do things like that, and I believe that when opportunities arise for you to do good, you should do good."[10]

Underwood also "did good" when finding a Christian mate. She met Mike Fisher, a former National Hockey League player for the Ottawa Senators and Nashville Predators in 2008 at a backstage meet-and-greet after one of her concerts, and they married in 2010. The couple has two children and openly speak about the importance of raising them as Christians. Every night they read Bible stories to their two sons, Isaiah and Jacob (did you catch those names?), and attend church as a family every week.

In 2020, the couple launched a television series called *Mike and Carrie: God & Country*, discussing how their faith has helped them in their marriage and kept them centered.

In 2021, Underwood recorded her first album of gospel hymns. *My Savior* consisted of those Underwood grew up singing ("Jesus

Loves Me," "Just As I Am," "How Great Thou Art," etc.) and featured a duet ("Great Is Thy Faithfulness") with CCM star CeCe Winans. Underwood's label, Capitol Records Nashville, went big by releasing *My Savior* digitally, on compact disc, and on vinyl simultaneously, as well as offering it as a limited-edition boxed set.

Underwood said the album was her way of deepening her relationship with Christ.

"When I made this album, I'm performing for an audience of one. I'm gonna cry talking about it, but . . . The whole time I was in the studio, any time I get to sing these songs, I close my eyes and I'm the only person in the room," Underwood said. "It's my heart for God. And I love that. It is a different feeling. It's happy and it's deep. And I feel like I'm making my relationship better and deeper with God when I'm singing these songs. So, they're just so important for my heart."[11]

God clearly rewarded her efforts. *My Savior* debuted at the top of the *Billboard* Country Album chart, as well as the *Billboard* Christian Album chart in May 2021. Carrie Underwood's life is unique and exemplary because she's chosen to live for Jesus Christ.

• • •

Like Underwood, Jordin Sparks grew up in a Christian home. And two years after Underwood, she too rose to fame because of *American Idol.* She was seventeen, the youngest winner in the show's history.

Her debut album, released later that year, went platinum and sold more than two million copies worldwide. It spawned two *Billboard* Hot 100 top-ten singles: "Tattoo" and "No Air." The latter song earned Sparks her first Grammy nomination. She was officially a famous musician.

But that's all she was. She admits she had no other identity. She grew up as a Christian but did not live that way.

"After a while, my behavior made me feel like a zombie and I wasn't sure of who I was," she said. "And that wasn't working for me."[12] So she gave her life to Jesus on Easter Sunday 2016.

She performed for us at our church the next Easter Sunday, and also joined me for one of our Harvest events in a stadium in Arizona.

"It wasn't until I was completely broken and torn that Jesus poured His love on me," she said.[13] "Everything shifted, and my perspective totally changed. It changed the things I said 'yes' to and the things I said 'no' to, and it made me realize that my joy doesn't come from this world. My joy comes from Jesus and knowing that if all of this fell away, if I lost everything, I'd still be okay."[14]

Now Sparks encourages people to fully entrust their lives to God.

"He's been so faithful to me and never abandoned me," she said. "I know He will do the same for you."[15]

Her life has changed dramatically. She still struggles with things, but even in her low moments, she knows she is in God's hands.

"I am different in so many ways, such as having a peace that I have never had before in my entire life and a joy that nobody can take away," she said.[16]

Every person takes their own unique journey through life. It's filled with experiences joyous and difficult, easy and painful, Sparks likes to say.

"But somewhere along the line, after many experiences, they finally 'wake up,'" she said. "I love the expression: 'when a man's Bible is falling apart, the man isn't.'"[17]

• • •

Like Underwood, Kendrick Lamar didn't come to his faith through a spectacular fall or losing everything. He just never went in that direction in the first place, although he has had every opportunity.

No top-billing rapper is more vocal about his personal religious beliefs than Lamar. He's an anomaly among rappers: despite being a platinum-selling artist, he is too secular for Christian audiences (even a brief peek at his lyrics is enough to peel your eyelids back), and he's too Christian for secular crowds. Every one of his albums tells the story of some sort of spiritual journey. He is an enigma.

You're probably not going to see him on TMZ; he doesn't go to strip clubs; he married his high school girlfriend before becoming famous. His biggest vice is his love for Fruity Pebbles. And he once dressed as Jesus for Halloween—make of that what you will.

He credits God with delivering him from the black hole of crime and violence in Compton, California, where he grew up in the 1990s. He doesn't glamorize the street life he avoided in his teens. He has never wanted to perform stereotypical rap music, and he told the *New York Times* in 2015 no one living around crime and drug dealing wants to hear it, either.

"They want to get away from that," he said. "If it comes across as just a game all the time, the kids are going to think it's just a game."[18]

Lamar's family was on welfare and lived in Section 8 housing; his father was a former gang member. But Lamar was quiet and shy, earning straight As in high school. His family didn't attend church, but his grandmother exposed him to biblical teachings.

He claims to have been baptized twice, though he's never aligned himself with a particular church or denomination. The first was after someone he knew was murdered in Compton. A friend's grandmother approached Lamar in a Food 4 Less parking lot, asking him if he had accepted Christ; the teenaged Lamar then prayed to receive Jesus. He was baptized again in 2013, an event he announced publicly during a concert.

Lamar got his start rapping as a teenager. He released a mixtape which sold well in Los Angeles. Between 2004 and 2012, he paid his industry dues—collaborating and performing with other artists, climbing the ladder all the way, and getting noticed by the right people.

When his album *Good Kid, M.A.A.D City* was released in 2012 to critical acclaim, it went platinum and hit number one on the *Billboard* 200. It opens with these words:

> *Lord God, I come to You a sinner, and I humbly repent for my sins. I believe that Jesus is Lord. I believe that You raised Him from the dead. I will ask that Jesus will come into my life and be my Lord and Savior. I receive Jesus to take control of my life, that I may live for Him from this day forth. Thank you, Lord Jesus, for saving me with Your precious blood. In Jesus's name, amen.*

Lamar's fourth album—*DAMN*—produced a *Billboard* Hot 100 single in 2017. It was the first non-classical and non-jazz album to win the Pulitzer Prize for Music. According to History.com, this was "a sign of the American cultural elite's recognition of hip-hop as a legitimate artistic medium."

In 2018, Lamar wrote and produced fourteen songs for the soundtrack of the Marvel Comics superhero film *Black Panther*. He puts in long hours in the studio—alone, without an entourage.

He has been known to turn his phone off for weeks at a time while deep in a project.

Lamar says his career is divinely inspired.

"I got a greater purpose," he said. "God put something in my heart to get across and that's what I'm going to focus on, using my voice as an instrument and doing what needs to be done."[19]

His spirituality has not come from being at the bottom of a bottle of bourbon or a pile of cocaine for years; it comes from having witnessed real sin, like seeing his uncle murdered when he was five years old.

In 2017, Lamar wrote an email to the music news website DJBooth after it ran a series of articles on him; the site then published it in full. He wrote about having recently attended a church service where the pastor spoke about hope:

> I've finally figured out why I left those (church) services feeling spiritually unsatisfied as a child. I discovered more truth. But simple truth. Our God is a loving God. Yes. He's a merciful God. Yes. But he's even more so a God of DISCIPLINE. OBEDIENCE. A JEALOUS God. And for every conscious choice of sin, will be corrected through his discipline.[20]
>
> As a community, we was taught to pray for our mishaps, and He'll forgive you. Yes, this is true. But He will also reprimand us as well. As a child, I can't recall hearing this in service. Maybe leaders of the church knew it will run off churchgoers? We want to hear about hope, salvation, and redemption. Though His son died for our sins, our free will to make whatever choice we want, still allows him to judge us.[21]

So in conclusion, I feel it's my calling to share the joy of
God, but with exclamation, more so, the FEAR OF GOD.
The balance. Knowing the power in what He can build,
and also what He can destroy. At any given moment.[22]

• • •

Today, our world seems dark and dingy compared to days gone
by. Yet these twenty-first-century artists are onto something that
brightens our world. They exhibit excitement about their futures
because of their faith in Jesus. Although they have seen and experienced a lot of what the world has had to offer, they've found
nothing that compares to the tangible new life and hope they have
in Christ.

In fact, the Bible reminds us to "always be prepared to give an
answer to everyone who asks you to give the reason about the hope
you have" (1 Peter 3:15 NIV). This verse tells us that we must
always be ready to tell others the good news of redemption through
faith. It must be presented with gentleness, respect, and without
harshness.

The Bible tells us nothing compares to the glory of Heaven—a
place of great beauty that is completely devoid of evil. We will all
enjoy meaningful work there. We will experience no more tears of
sorrow, death, or pain—only life eternally filled with love, hope,
and beauty. Those will be our Glory Days.

Thank God for the genuine life experiences of these young
musicians who are bold enough to stand firmly on God's promises
and not get caught up in the frivolity and insecurity of a false fame
and fortune.

Some of them have had it quite easy, like Carrie Underwood
and Jordin Sparks. Some, like Rudy Sarzo and Kendrick Lamar,

have never had any doubts about their personal faith. Others, like Alice Cooper, Brian Welch, and Justin Bieber, had to fall into the abyss before they were able to crawl out with God's help. Even dabblers like John Lennon came away with truths.

This is the heart of God. He is calling out to humanity saying, "Come! Come to Me!"

And what will happen when we come? Our spiritual hunger will be satisfied, and our spiritual thirst will be quenched. Revelation 22:17 is an invitation. It isn't a summons. It isn't anything forced. It's not, "Come to Me—or else!"

"Whoever desires, let him take the water of life freely," God is saying. "If you want a drink from the water of life, the living water that will save you from Hell and a wasted life on Earth, just come on and take it. If you don't want it, you don't have to. This is an offer I extend to all of humanity."

Deep down inside, every one of us is thirsty for something more in life—things this world simply cannot give us. It won't come through a relationship. It won't come through our possessions. It won't come through our accomplishments or fame. It won't come through some exhilarating experience. All these things will leave us empty. That's because we are thirsting for God Himself.

A doctor named Robin L. Smith wrote a book called *Hungry: The Truth About a Satisfied Soul*. In it, she writes about those who feel emptiness after experiencing great success and calls it "being hungry for the high note." Smith maintains that Michael Jackson and Whitney Houston, both of whom died around the age of fifty, weren't killed by drugs per se—even though they both used them. In fact, Houston said before she died, "I'm going to hit that high note again."

So you hit a high note. You're at the peak of life. But what then? You can't hold that high note anymore. You're not as successful as you once were, and you can't bear that. That's why so many of these super successful people end up strung out on drugs or alcohol. But drugs and alcohol aren't the real issue; emptiness is.

When you think about it, God could have chosen to wrap up the Bible in any of several ways, but He chose to end it with an invitation to anyone who feels empty and thirsts for something more than they've ever found in life. He simply says, "Come."

How do you come to Jesus? It starts with a prayer—a very simple prayer in which you move your heart toward God.

The Bible states, "Everyone who calls on the name of the Lord will be saved" (Romans 10:13 NIV).

This reminds me of a story from many years ago.

I was in the ocean, helping my young son, Jonathan, try to catch some waves. Suddenly, I was caught in a mild riptide and lost my footing. I was trying to keep Jonathan above the water, and I was struggling. A very alert lifeguard spotted me and began to run in my direction. I really did not want to be "saved," because I was only a few feet from shore. But the fact remained that I was in a riptide.

Fortunately, I was able to plant my feet on the sand and tell the lifeguard, "Thanks, I'm okay." Frankly, I was too proud to be saved. After all, I was raised near the ocean and I knew what I was doing, right?

Or did I?

That's how a lot of us are when it comes to God: we are too proud to be saved.

Some of us must hit bottom, like many of the people I wrote about in this book. But if you are one of them, I want you to know that God is only a prayer away.

You can have a second chance in life and be free from whatever addiction has a hold on you. Best of all, you can be forgiven of all your sins and know that when you die, you will go to Heaven.

If you would like this second chance in life, please pray this prayer:

Lord Jesus . . .

I know that I am a sinner.

But I know that You are the Savior who died on the cross for my sins and rose again from the dead.

Lord, I am sorry for my sins, and I repent of them now.

Come into my life. I choose to follow You from this day forward as my Savior, my Lord, my God, and my Friend. Thank You for hearing and answering this prayer.

In Jesus's name I pray.

Amen.

If you prayed that prayer, I want you to know that Christ has come into your life! Congratulations, and welcome to the family of God.

If you send me an email at Greg@Harvest.org, I will send you at no charge something called *The New Believer's Bible*. It's a very understandable translation with hundreds of notes I wrote that will encourage you in this new commitment you have made. I look forward to hearing from you.

Greg Laurie

Acknowledgements

This was an unusual and fascinating book to write, but make no mistake—a lot of hard work and research went into this project. *Lennon, Dylan, Alice, & Jesus* spans six decades of music, pop culture, and history. Trying to make sense of each era while delivering a specific point of view is a delicate balancing act. I have tried to be even-handed and let the stories unfold as they did and, in some cases, they are still a work in progress. The artists we have explored are fascinating and extraordinarily talented people. They influence others. But when the day is done, they are pretty much like you and me, trying to figure out life and its meaning.

First and foremost, I'd like to thank Marshall Terrill. This is the fourth book that we have done together. Marshall is a master researcher and fantastic writer. He is also a great collaborator. I could not have done this book without him.

I also want to thank Scott Seckel, our talented developmental editor, for his hours of dedication, guiding hand, and wisdom; and Cara Highsmith, also a talented editor who "sweetens" the final mix with her eagle eye. Then there's Karla Dial of Salem Books, who has the final say and gives the manuscript a deft touch where it's needed.

Speaking of Salem, they are a wonderful literary partner; this is my third endeavor with them. Salem is everything you could ask for in a publisher and more. In addition to Karla, their team includes Tim Peterson, Jennifer Valk, Katie Anderson, and Kim Lilienthal.

Thanks must also be given to Erik and Robert Wolgemuth, my literary agents. Things are always smooth when left in their capable hands. They take the worry out of the work and make it a real joy.

A tip of the hat must go to my wife of forty-eight years, Cathe Laurie. She often sacrifices her time with me so I can pursue my literary, documentary, and movie endeavors. But wherever I am and whatever I do, she is right there by my side.

Lastly, I thank the Harvest congregation and our friends who follow our ministry around the world. It is an honor to serve you and our Lord Jesus Christ.

Notes

Chapter One

1. Sonny West and Marshall Terrill, *Elvis: Still Taking Care of Business* (Chicago: Triumph Books, 2007), 17.
2. Alanna Nash with Billy Smith, Marty Lacker, and Lamar Fike, *Elvis Aaron Presley: Revelations from the Memphis Mafia* (New York: HarperCollins, 1995), 18.
3. Helyn Trickey, "Gospel Music and Elvis: Inspiration and Consolation," CNN, August 14, 2002, http://www.cnn.com/2002/SHOWBIZ/Music/08/14/ep.elvis.gospel/.
4. Greg Laurie and Marshall Terrill, *Johnny Cash: The Redemption of an American Icon* (Washington, D.C.: Salem Books, 2019), 30.
5. Douglas Martin, "Sam Phillips, Who Discovered Elvis Presley, Dies at 80," *New York Times*, August 1, 2003.
6. Elvis Australia, "Roy Orbison Talks about Elvis Presley and 'Only the Lonely,'" YouTube, February 26, 2016, https://www.youtube.com/watch?v=YKWX98SoIKA.
7. Eric Meisfjord, "The Real Reason Elvis Presley Covered Blue Suede Shoes by Carl Perkins," Grunge, June 17, 2020, https://www.grunge.com/218599/the-real-reason-elvis-presley-covered-blue-suede-shoes-by-carl-perkins/.

8. Gary Tillery, *The Seeker King: A Spiritual Biography of Elvis Presley* (Wheaton, IL: Quest Books, 2012), 3.

9. Thom Zimny, *Elvis Presley: The Searcher*, HBO, 2018.

10. Ibid.

11. West, *Elvis: Still Taking Care of Business*, 275.

12. Laurie, *Johnny Cash: The Redemption of an American Icon*, 71.

13. Carl Perkins with Ron Rendleman, *Disciple in Blue Suede Shoes* (Grand Rapids, MI: Zondervan, 1978), 15.

14. Carl Perkins and David McGee, *Go Cat, Go!* (New York: Hyperion, 1996), 311.

15. Bobby Copeland, "When 'The Killer' Came to Oakridge," *Oak Ridger*, December 17, 2013.

16. Simon Hattenstone, "Jerry Lee Lewis: I Worry about Whether or Not I'm Going to Heaven or Hell," *The Guardian*, August 8, 2015.

Chapter Two

1. Maureen Cleeve, "How Does a Beatle Live?" *Evening Standard*, March 4, 1966.

2. Jean Shepherd, "A Candid Conversation with England's Mop-Topped Millionaire Minstrels," *Playboy*, February 1965.

3. The Beatles, *Anthology* (San Francisco: Chronicle Books, 2000), 171.

4. Olivia Harrison, *George Harrison: Living in the Material World* (New York: Abrams, 2011), 216.

5. Luka Simonetti, "Check Out This Rare Psychedelic Footage of Ravi Shankar Teaching George Harrison the Sitar," Happy, April 14, 2020, https://happymag.tv/check-out-this-rare-psychedelic-footage-of-ravi-shankar-teaching-george-harrison-the-sitar/.

6. Jordan Runtah, "Beatles' 'Sgt. Pepper' at 50: How George Harrison Found Himself on 'Within You Without You,'" *Rolling Stone*, May 25, 2017.

7. The Beatles, *Anthology*, 258.

8. Ken Mansfield, personal interview, May 16, 2020.

9. Jonathan Cott, "John Lennon: The Rolling Stone Interview," *Rolling Stone*, November 23, 1968.

10. The Beatles, *Anthology*, 285.

11. Chris O'Dell, *Miss O'Dell: My Hard Days and Long Nights with The Beatles, The Stones, Bob Dylan, Eric Clapton, and the Women They Loved* (New York: Touchstone, 2009), 154.

12. Randy Lewis and Dennis Hunt, "Hollywood Star Walk," *Los Angeles Times*, July 7, 2008.

13. David Lister, "Paul McCartney Talks Jimmy Savile and (Unusually for Him) the Real John Lennon," *The Independent*, November 23, 2012.

14. Mary Louise Kelly, "'It Becomes More and More Special': Paul McCartney on His Friendship with John Lennon," NPR, December 11, 2020.

15. William Glaberson, "Beatles' Estate Sues Doctor over Breach of Privacy," *New York Times*, January 7, 2014.

Chapter Three

1. Sean Moores, "Patriotism or Protest? Army Vet Jimi Hendrix Had the 'Most Electrifying Moment' at Woodstock," *Stars & Stripes*, August 15, 2019.

2. Justin Chandler, "'It's Like a Religion': Listen to Jimi Hendrix Describe His Music in This 1969 CBC Interview," CBC, November 27, 2018, https://www.cbc.ca/music/it-s-like-a-religion-listen-to-jimi-hendrix-describe-his-music-in-this-1969-cbc-interview-1.5037424.

3. Robert Draper, "O Janis," *Texas Monthly*, October 1992.

4. Alan Paul, "The Doors' Robby Krieger Sheds Light—Album by Album—on One of Rock's Most Mysterious Bands," *Guitar World*, January 8, 2016.

5. Paul Ferrara, *Feast of Friends*, Eagle Rock Entertainment, 2014.

6. "Dawn's Highway a Short Documentary Film Uncovers Witnesses, Actual Site of 'Dawn's Highway' Accident," PR Newswire, August 9, 2016, https://www.prnewswire.com/news-releases/dawns-highway-a-short-documentary-film-uncovers-witnesses-actual-site-of-dawns-highway-accident-300310915.html.

7. Dee Norton, Peyton Whitely, Dave Birkland, and Barbara Serrano, "Nirvana's Cobain Dead—Suicide Note, Shotgun near Body of Musician at His Seattle Home—Mother: 'Now He's Gone and Joined That Stupid Club,'" *Seattle Times*, April 8, 1994.

8. Sarah Weissman, "5 Facts about Amy Winehouse's Jewish Roots: She Hated Hebrew School, Loved Family Celebrations," *Washington Post*, July 23, 2015.

9. Kyle Anderson, "Tony Bennett on Amy Winehouse: 'She Was Very Nervous' Recording 'Body & Soul,'" *Entertainment Weekly*, September 9, 2011.

10. Tyler James, "Amy Winehouse 'Was Barely Conscious after Five Days' Solid Drinking but They Picked Her off the Sofa and Put Her in a Car to Go On Tour': Ten Years after Her Death, the Singer's Best Friend Tyler James Raises Tough Questions for Music Industry," *Daily Mail*, May 22, 2021.

11. Ken Mansfield and Marshall Terrill, *Rock and a Heart Place* (Racine, WI: BroadStreet Publishing Group, 2015), 179.

12. Chloe Melas, "Avicii's Family Reveals His Personal Struggles in New Statement," CNN, April 27, 2018, https://www.cnn.com/2018/04/26/entertainment/avicii-family-statement/index.html.

Chapter Four

1. Terry Mattingly, "Larry Norman and the Never-Ending Culture Wars over 'Christian' Music and Art," *Knoxville News Sentinel*, April 21, 2018.

2. Marshall Terrill, *The Jesus Music: A Visual Story of Redemption as Told by Those Who Lived It* (Rocklin, CA: K-LOVE Books, 2021), 38.

3. Jon and Andy Erwin, *The Jesus Music*, Lionsgate, 2021.

4. Terrill, *The Jesus Music: A Visual Story of Redemption as Told by Those Who Lived It*, 39.

5. A new feature film that tells the story of this last great spiritual awakening, titled *Jesus Revolution*, will release next year in theaters everywhere.

Chapter Five

1. Scott Marshall, *Bob Dylan: A Spiritual Life* (Hawthorne, NV: WND Books, 2017), 15.

2. Ibid., 219.

3. Ibid., 30.

4. J-P Mauro, "Bob Dylan's 'Trouble No More: Faith-Filled Music from His Gospel Period," Aleteia, January 5, 2018, https://aleteia.

org/2018/01/05/trouble-no-more-bob-dylans-conversion-began-with-a-little-silver-cross.

5. Andrew McCarron, "The Year Bob Dylan Was Born Again: A Timeline," Oxford University Press blog, January 17, 2021, https://blog.oup.com/2017/01/bob-dylan-christianity.

6. Nadine Epstein and Rebecca Frankel, "Bob Dylan: The Unauthorized Spiritual Biography," *Moment*, July–August 2005.

7. Jennifer Goetz, personal interview, September 2, 2021.

8. Marshall, *Bob Dylan: A Spiritual Life*, 43.

9. Jennifer Goetz, personal interview, September 2, 2021.

10. Ezra Klein, "Jimmy Carter's 'Malaise Speech' Was Popular!" *Washington Post*, August 9, 2013.

11. CB Condez, "Bob Dylan's '80s Letter Auctioned, Gives Glimpse into Artist's Christian Faith," *Christian Times*, May 20, 2016.

12. Yo Zushi, "Bob Dylan and His Vengeful, Conservative God," *New Statesman*, November 9, 2017.

13. Andy Greene, "Bob Dylan's New Bootleg Series Will Spotlight Gospel Period," *Rolling Stone*, September 20, 2017.

14. Richard Williams, "Bob Dylan's Controversial Born-Again Phase Explored in New Film," *The Guardian*, March 16, 2016.

15. Kurt Loder, "Bob Dylan, Recovering Christian," *Rolling Stone*, June 21, 1984.

16. Marshall, *Bob Dylan: A Spiritual Life*, 188.

17. Michael J. Gilmour, *The Gospel According to Bob Dylan: The Old, Old Story for Modern Times* (Louisville: Westminster John Knox Press, 2011), 43.

18. Marshall, *Bob Dylan: A Spiritual Life*, 237–38.

Chapter Six

1. Toni Klein, *Fairies: An Informative and Whimsical Guide* (Bloomington, IN: iUniverse, 2018), 4.

2. Ivor Davis, personal interview, June 14, 2021.

3. Pete Hamill, "John Lennon: Long Night's Journey into Day," *Rolling Stone*, June 5, 1975.

4. Oral Roberts University, December 1972.

5. Anthony DeCurtis, "His Kind of Shellshocked Town," *New York Times*, May 17, 2009.

6. Robert Rosen, personal interview, July 9, 2021.

7. Ibid.

8. Ibid.

9. Carol Fleenor, "I Saw Him Standing There," *Guideposts*, September 1, 2008, https://www.guideposts.org/better-living/entertainment/music/i-saw-him-standing-there.

10. Ibid.

11. Ibid.

12. Ibid.

13. Ibid.

14. Ibid.

15. Ibid.

16. Robert Rosen, personal interview, July 9, 2021.

17. Kenneth Womack, "John Lennon Sailed to Bermuda through a Storm, 'Screaming Sea Shanties and Shouting at the Gods,'" Salon, July 11, 2020, https://www.salon.com/2020/07/11/john-lennon-sailed-to-bermuda-through-a-storm-screaming-sea-shanties-and-shouting-at-the-gods/.

18. Ibid

19. Ibid.

20. Sean Braswell, "When John Lennon Almost Sailed to His Death," OZY, September 23, 2017, https://www.ozy.com/true-and-stories/when-john-lennon-almost-sailed-to-his-death/80816/.

21. Robert Knight, "Left-Wing Activist Kevin Powell Wants to Replace 'Star-Spangled Banner' with John Lennon's 'Imagine,'" *Washington Times*, July 3, 2020.

22. Colin Stutz, "Paul McCartney Says, 'John Lennon's Whole Life Was a Cry for Help,'" *Billboard*, November 12, 2015.

23. Robert Rosen, personal interview, July 9, 2021.

Chapter Seven

1. Richie Furay with Michael Roberts, *Pickin' Up the Pieces: The Heart and Soul of Country Rock Pioneer Richie Furay* (Colorado Springs: WaterBrook Press, 2006), 55.

2. Ken Mansfield and Marshall Terrill, *Rock and a Heart Place* (Racine, WI: BroadStreet Publishing Group, 2015), 280.

3. Pamela Danzinger, "Meet Roger McGuinn, Working Musician and Man of Faith," Faith Underground, December 5, 2018, https://faithunderground.org/2018/12/05/meet-roger-mcguinn-working-musician-and-man-of-faith/.

4. Ibid.

5. Chris Hillman, *Time Between: My Life as a Byrd, Burrito Brother, and Beyond* (Berlin: BMG, 2020), 172.
6. Mansfield, *Rock and a Heart Place*, 102.
7. Ibid., 254.
8. Furay, *Pickin' Up the Pieces*, 144.
9. Ibid., 203.
10. Scott Ross, "Lou Gramm Knows What Love Is," CBN, March 2, 2014, https://www1.cbn.com/content/lou-gramm-knows-what-love-extended-version?show=700club.
11. Ibid.
12. Dennis Hunt, "Two Kansans Find God, Lower Economic Expectations," *Los Angeles Times*, December 18, 1980.
13. Kerry Livgren, *Miracles Out of Somewhere* (Numavox, 2020), 178.
14. Mansfield, *Rock and a Heart Place*, 284.
15. Ibid., 285.
16. "Born-Again Christian Donna Summer 'Very Sincere' about Her Faith Before Passing," EEWBUZZ, May 18, 2012, https://buzz. eewmagazine.com/eew-magazine-buzz-blog/2012/5/18/born-again-christian-donna-summer-very-sincere-about-her-fai.html.
17. Erica Thompson, "'Deliverance—Donna Summer + Prince Part II," A Purple Day in December blog, July 10, 2020, http://www. apurpledayindecember.com/2020/07/deliverance-donna-summer-prince-part-two.html.
18. Richard Harrington, "Donna Summer's Saving Grace," *Washington Post*, July 29, 1981.

Chapter Eight

1. Alice Cooper, personal interview, January 2019.
2. Ibid.
3. "Alice Cooper," SickThingsUK, https://www.sickthingsuk. co.uk/08-musicians/m-alice.php.
4. Ibid.
5. Alice Cooper, personal interview, January 2019.
6. Dave Thompson, *Alice Cooper: Welcome to My Nightmare* (London: Omnibus Press, 2012), 40.
7. Alice Cooper, personal interview, January 2019.
8. Ibid.
9. Ibid.

10. Roy Hollingsworth, "Ladies and Gentlemen, You've Seen Him Electrocuted, You've Seen Him Hung, and Now You're about to See Him Fired from a Cannon. Yes, Ladies and Gentlemen, Alice Cooper!" *Melody Maker*, July 1, 1972.

11. Benya Clark, "Why Alice Cooper Got Sober," Medium, May 21, 2020, https://medium.com/exploring-sobriety/why-alice-cooper-got-sober-239b3e1b652c.

12. Lyndsay Parker, "Alice Cooper Talks Early-'80s 'Blackout Albums': 'The Coke Had Done Its Damage,'" Yahoo! Entertainment, July 2, 2020, https://www.yahoo.com/video/alice-cooper-talks-early-80-s-blackout-albums-the-coke-had-done-its-damage-214001856.html.

13. Martin Kielty, "Pastor Told Alice Cooper to Keep Being Alice Cooper," Ultimate Classic Rock, August 22, 2019, https://ultimateclassicrock.com/alice-cooper-pastor-advice/.

14. Alice Cooper, personal interview, January 2019.

15. Ibid.

16. Ibid.

Chapter Nine

1. Michael Friedman, "The Middle Finger Effect of Dee Snider," Psychology Today blog, July 26, 2018, https://www.psychologytoday.com/us/blog/brick-brick/201807/the-middle-finger-factor-dee-snider.

2. "Dee Snider's PMRC Senate Hearing Speech," YouTube, May 4, 2012, https://www.youtube.com/watch?v=SoVyr1TylTE.

3. Deb, "Interview with Blackie Lawless of W.A.S.P.," Ear Candy, May 20, 2001, http://earcandy_mag.tripod.com/wasp.htm, accessed Nov. 22, 2021.

4. Joe DiVita, "How Blackie Lawless Went from F – ing like a Beast to Smiting the Beast," LoudWire, February 22, 2018, https://loudwire.com/w-a-s-p-blackie-lawless-f-king-like-a-beast-smiting-beast/.

5. Ibid.

6. Ken Mansfield and Marshall Terrill, *Rock and a Heart Place* (Racine, WI: BroadStreet Publishing Group, 2015), 139.

7. Rudy Sarzo, *Off the Rails: Aboard the Crazy Train in the Blizzard of Ozz* (Scotts Valley, CA: CreateSpace, 2016), 269.

8. Mansfield, *Rock and a Heart Place*, 144.

9. Ibid., 146.
10. Bill Blankenship, "C. C. DeVille: 'I Was Addicted to Drugs, Everything Was Based around the Drugs,'" *Topeka-Capital Journal*, June 23, 2000.
11. Ibid.
12. "Poison Guitarist C. C. DeVille: 'I'm Learning Grace from the Lord,'" Blabbermouth.net, August 1, 2008, https://www.blabbermouth.net/news/poison-guitarist-c-c-deville-i-m-learning-grace-from-the-lord.
13. Ibid.
14. "Dave Mustaine: 'I Would Have Kicked Me Out of Metallica,'" Metal Hammer, October 11, 2016, https://www.loudersound.com/features/dave-mustaine-megadth-interview-drugs-politics-religion-metallica.
15. Joe Wiederhorn, "38 Years Ago: Dave Mustaine Fired from Metallica," Loudwire, April 11, 2021, https://loudwire.com/dave-mustaine-fired-from-metallica-anniversary.
16. Nestor Aparicio, "Megadeth's Dave Mustaine Says Hard Living Is behind Him," *Baltimore Evening Sun*, June 27, 1991.
17. Ibid.
18. Graham Hartmann, "Dave Mustaine: 'I Have a Personal Relationship with Christ' but I Don't Believe In Religion," Loudwire, September 14, 2013, https://loudwire.com/dave-mustaine-personal-relationship-with-christ-dont-believe-in-religion/.

Chapter Ten

1. Brian Welch, *Save Me From Myself: How I Found God, Quit Korn, Kicked Drugs, and Lived to Tell My Story* (New York: HarperCollins, 2009), 16.
2. Ibid., 20.
3. Ken Mansfield and Marshall Terrill, *Rock and a Heart Place* (Racine, WI: BroadStreet Publishing Group, 2015), 65.
4. Ibid., 75.
5. Tim Branson, "Korn Bassist Fieldy on the Christian Life," CBN, November 15, 2010, https://www1.cbn.com/video/korn-bassist-fieldy-on-the-christian-life.

6. Ibid.

7. Fieldy with Laura Morton, *Got the Life: My Journey of Addiction, Faith, Recovery and Korn* (New York: HarperCollins, 2009), 96.

8. Branson, "Korn Bassist Fieldy on the Christian Life."

9. Ibid.

10. Fieldy, *Got the Life: My Journey of Addiction, Faith, Recovery and Korn*, 218.

11. Tony Cummings, "Shelia E: World Acclaimed Drummer and Singer and a Witness for Christ," Cross Rhythms, January 1, 2014, https://www.crossrhythms.co.uk/articles/music/Sheila_E_World_acclaimed_drummer_and_singer_and_a_witness_for_Christ/52881/p1/.

12. Sheila E. with Wendy Holden, *The Beat of My Own Drum* (New York: Atria Books, 2014), 253.

13. Ibid., 254.

14. Cummings, "Sheila E."

15. Sheila E., *The Beat of My Own Drum*, 260.

16. "Scott Stapp on faithvillage.com," ScottStapp.com, quoted from Faithvillage.com, December 5, 2012, https://scottstapp.com/news/115191.

17. Joe D'Angelo, "Scott Stapp Breaks His Silence," MTV, August 9, 2004.

18. Shirley Halperin, "Scott Stapp and 311 Brawl," *Rolling Stone*, December 1, 2005.

19. Robert Kessler, "Creed's Scott Stapp Admits He Has a Bipolar Disorder," Yahoo! Entertainment, May 13, 2015, https://www.yahoo.com/entertainment/blogs/celeb-news/creed-s-scott-stapp-says-he-has-bipolar-disorder-125551654.html.

20. "Scott Stapp on faithvillage.com."

21. "Why Stars Go Broke," *Ebony*, May 1998.

22. Margaret Ramirez, "Voicing His Faith," *Los Angeles Times*, February 19, 2000.

Chapter Eleven

1. "EP" stands for "extended play." It is an album that usually contains four to five songs and is typically used when an artist doesn't have enough material for a full album but wants to put it

out when they are hit with a bout of inspiration, or to tide fans over with new material.

2. Justin Bieber, Instagram post, September 6, 2020, https://www.instagram.com/p/CEoMOIVHXjp/?hl=en.

3. Hannah Yasharhoff, "Justin Bieber Gets Candid about Past Drug Addiction, Getting Sober: I 'Felt Like I Was Dying,'" *USA Today*, February 4, 2020, https://www.usatoday.com/story/entertainment/celebrities/2020/02/04/justin-bieber-drug-addiction-detailed-waking-up-popping-pills-getting-sober/4653541002.

4. Ibid.

5. Zach Baron, "The Redemption of Justin Bieber," *GQ*, April 13, 2021.

6. Ibid.

7. Drew Weisholtz, "Justin Bieber Shares Pictures of the Moment He and Wife Hailey Got Baptized," Yahoo! News, August 6, 2020, https://www.yahoo.com/now/justin-bieber-shares-pictures-moment-125319633.html.

8. Kathryn Post, "Justin Bieber's Easter Surprise EP, 'Freedom,' Adds to His Jesus-Filled Chapter," Religion News Service, April 7, 2021, https://religionnews.com/2021/04/07/justin-biebers-easter-surprise-ep-freedom-adds-to-his-jesus-filled-chapter/.

9. Michelle Miller, "Carrie Underwood's Gospel Gifts," CBS News This Morning, Saturday, April 4, 2021, https://www.cbsnews.com/news/carrie-underwood-album-of-gospel-standards-my-savior.

10. Joe McCarthy, "Singer-Songwriter Carrie Underwood Wants to Change the World with Acts of Kindness," Global Citizen, December 15, 2020, https://www.globalcitizen.org/en/content/carrie-underwood-kindness-global-citizen-prize/.

11. Minni Elkins, "Carrie Underwood's 'My Savior' Tops Billboard Chart: Singing the Old Hymns to an Audience of One," Denison Forum, April 15, 2021, https://www.denisonforum.org/columns/entertainment/carrie-underwoods-my-savior-tops-billboard-chart-singing-the-old-hymns-to-an-audience-of-one/.

12. "'Jesus Poured His Love on Me': Jordin Sparks Reveals How God Changed Her from Feeling 'Like a Zombie,'" CBN, December 4, 2017, https://www1.cbn.com/cbnnews/entertainment/2017/december/jesus-poured-his-love-on-me-jordin-sparks-reveals-how-god-changed-her-from-feeling-like-a-zombie.

13. Ibid.
14. MarieAnn Klett, "Jordin Sparks Shares How Birth of Son Re-Inspired Her Christian Faith," *Christian Post*, September 6, 2018, https://www.christianpost.com/news/jordin-sparks-prayer-newborn-son-birth-strengthened-faith-christ.html.
15. "'Jesus Poured His Love on Me': Jordin Sparks Reveals How God Changed Her from Feeling 'Like a Zombie.'"
16. Ibid.
17. Czarina Ong, "Jordin Sparks Shares Her Love for the Bible: 'These Are So Much More than Words,'" *Christianity Today*, December 16, 2016, https://www.christiantoday.com/article/jordin-sparks-shares-her-love-for-the-bible-these-are-so-much-more-than-words/103041.htm.
18. Joe Coscarelli, "Kendrick Lamar on His New Album and the Weight of Clarity," *New York Times*, March 16, 2015.
19. Insanul Ahmed, "Turn the Page," *Complex*, August-September 2012.
20. Tyler Huckabee, "Hip-Hop Is Having a God Moment: Kendrick Lamar Is a Big Part of It," *Washington Post*, January 28, 2018.
21. Carly Hoilman, "Grammy-Winning Rapper Calls Out Churches for Not Preaching the 'Hard Truth' of God's Judgment," Faithwire, May 5, 2017, https://www.faithwire.com/2017/11/28/grammy-winning-rapper-calls-out-churches-for-not-preaching-the-hard-truth-of-gods-judgment.
22. Stacy-Ann Ellis, "Kendrick Lamar: 'It's My Calling to Share the Joy of God, but More So the Fear of God,'" VIBE, April 28, 2017.

Selected Bibliography

Beatles, The. *Anthology*. San Francisco: Chronicle Books, 2000.

Burger, Jeff. *Lennon on Lennon: Conversations with John Lennon*. Chicago: Chicago Review Press, 2017.

Fieldy with Laura Morton. *Got the Life: My Journey of Addiction, Faith, Recovery and Korn*. New York: HarperCollins, 2009.

Furay, Richie with Michael Roberts. *Pickin' Up the Pieces: The Heart and Soul of Country Rock Pioneer Richie Furay*. Colorado Springs: WaterBrook Press, 2006.

Girard, Chuck. *Rock & Roll Preacher*. Houston, TX: Worldwide Publishing Group, 2020.

Harrison, Olivia. *George Harrison: Living in the Material World*. New York: Abrams, 2011.

Hillman, Chris. *Time Between: My Life as a Byrd, Burrito Brother, and Beyond*. Berlin: BMG, 2020.

Klein, Toni. *Fairies: An Informative and Whimsical Guide*. Bloomington, IN: iUniverse, 2018.

Laurie, Greg and Ellen Vaughn. *Jesus Revolution: How God Transformed an Unlikely Generation and How He Can Do It Again Today*. Grand Rapids, MI: Baker Books, 2018.

Laurie, Greg and Marshall Terrill. *Johnny Cash: The Redemption of an American Icon*. Washington, D.C.: Salem Books, 2019.

Livgren, Kerry. *Miracles Out of Somewhere*. Numavox, 2020.

Madinger, Chip and Scott Raile. *Lennonology*. Chesterfield, MO: Open Your Books, 2015.

Mansfield, Ken and Marshall Terrill. *Rock and a Heart Place*. Racine, WI: BroadStreet Publishing Group, 2015.

Marshall, Scott. *Bob Dylan: A Spiritual Life*. BP Books, 2017.

Nash, Alanna with Billy Smith, Marty Lacker, and Lamar Fike. *Elvis Aaron Presley: Revelations from the Memphis Mafia*. New York: HarperCollins, 1995.

Norman, Philip. *John Lennon: The Life*. New York: Ecco, 2008.

O'Dell, Chris. *Miss O'Dell: My Hard Days and Long Nights with The Beatles, The Stones, Bob Dylan, Eric Clapton, and the Women They Loved*. New York: Touchstone, 2009.

Perkins, Carl and David McGee. *Go, Cat, Go!* New York: Hyperion, 1996.

Perkins, Carl and Ron Rendleman. *Disciple in Blue Suede Shoes*. Grand Rapids, MI: Zondervan, 1978.

Rosen, Robert. *Nowhere Man: The Final Days of John Lennon*. New York: Soft Skull Press, 2000.

Saltzman, Paul. *The Beatles in Rishikesh*. London: Viking Studio, 2000.

Saimaru, Nishi. *The John Lennon Family Album*. San Francisco: Chronicle Books, 1982.

Sarzo, Rudy. *Off the Rails: Aboard the Crazy Train in the Blizzard of Ozz*. Scotts Valley, CA: CreateSpace, 2016.

Sheff, David. *All We Are Saying: The Last Major Interview with John Lennon and Yoko Ono.* New York: St. Martin's Griffin, 2010.

Sheila E. with Wendy Holden. *The Beat of My Own Drum.* New York: Atria Books, 2014.

Smith, Chuck. *Chuck Smith Autobiography: A Memoir of Grace.* Costa Mesa, CA: The Word for Today, 2009.

Stapp, Scott with David Ritz. *Sinner's Creed.* Carol Stream, IL: Tyndale, 2012.

Summer, Donna with Marc Eliot. *Ordinary Girl: The Journey.* New York: Villard, 2003.

Terrill, Marshall. *The Jesus Music: A Visual Story of Redemption As Told By Those Who Lived It.* Rocklin, CA: K-LOVE Books, 2021.

Thomson, Graeme. *George Harrison: Behind the Locked Door.* London: Omnibus Press, 2013.

Thompson, Dave. *Alice Cooper: Welcome to My Nightmare.* London: Omnibus Press, 2012.

Thornbury, Gregory Alan. *Why Should the Devil Have All the Good Music? Larry Norman and the Perils of Christian Rock.* New York: Convergent Books, 2018.

Tillery, Gary. *The Seeker King: A Spiritual Biography of Elvis Presley.* Wheaton, IL: Quest Books, 2013.

Trynka, Paul, ed. *The Beatles: 10 Years That Shook the World.* London: Dorling Kindersley, 2004.

Turner, Steve. *The Gospel According to the Beatles.* Louisville, KY: Westminster John Knox Press, 2006.

Welch, Brian. *Save Me from Myself: How I Found God, Quit Korn, Kicked Drugs, and Lived to Tell My Story.* New York: HarperCollins, 2009.

West, Sonny and Marshall Terrill. *Elvis: Still Taking Care of Business.* Chicago: Triumph Books, 2007.